Your School Leadership Edit

With this exciting book in hand, discover how to create an educational environment that maximizes focus, minimizes waste, and ultimately leads to a more sustainable and fulfilling experience for both students and staff! Advocating for an education of purpose and value, *Your School Leadership Edit* introduces educators to the transformative power of the 5R's in their school cultures: Reimagine, Remove, Repurpose, Reinvest, and Refine. Each chapter digs into practical strategies and dissects an essential aspect of minimalism, from building a people-centered culture to decluttering communication. With a focus on reshaping the purpose and culture of schools, this guide provides actionable and transformative insights for educators, administrators, and school leaders about how to do strategically less while also creating cultures of sustainable structures in their schools.

Additional Support Materials for this book are available for download at www.routledge.com/9781032936178

Tamera Musiowsky-Borneman is a Professional Development Coach for Catapult Learning and a Professional Learning Facilitator. She is an ASCD Emerging Leader Class of 2014, is the Executive Director of the Advancing Leaders Collaborative (ALC), and is a Hawai'i Society of Technology in Education (HSTE) Board Member.

C.Y. Arnold has worked in Australia, Japan, Singapore, Belgium, and the Netherlands as a Teacher, Coach, Mentor, Co-Teacher, Coordinator, Tutor, and Supervisor from early childhood education to adult education.

Also Available from Routledge Eye On Education
(www.routledge.com/eyeoneducation)

Game-Changing Leadership in Action: An Educator's Companion
Kim Wallace

How to Have Difficult Conversations as an Educational Leader: Self-Reflections and Strategies for Success
Patty Corum

The Respected School Leader: Developing your Character Traits and Transformational Leadership Skills
Howard J. Bultinck, Lynn H. Bush, Noreen A. Powers

The International Education Leadership Companion: Lessons and Best Practices from Expert Leaders
Lindsay Prendergast, Catarina Song Chen, Colin Brown

Leadership Teams in America's Best Schools: Improving the Lives of All Students
Joseph F. Johnson, Jr., Cynthia L. Uline, Stanley J. Munro, Jr., Francisco Escobedo

Making Community Schools a Reality: Harnessing Your Power as a School Leader through Collaboration
Emily L. Woods

Wholehearted School Leadership: Rewiring our Schools for Courage, Justice, Learning, and Connection
Kathryn Fishman-Weaver

Data Analysis for Continuous School Improvement, 5th Edition
Victoria L. Bernhardt

Culturally Conscious Decision-Making for School Leaders: A Toolkit for Creating a More Equitable School Culture
Shauna McGee

Teacher Leadership Practice in High-Performing Schools: A Blueprint for Excellence
Jeremy D. Visone

"Practically every person I know in a leadership position is overwhelmed by the "too many" demands they face in their roles. If that's you, and I bet it is, this is the book for you. This book will tell you how to declutter your relationships, your calendar, and give you insights into how to reimagine what school systems can look like when they are simplified and streamlined. This allows leaders to focus on what really matters. I know it's a book you're going to need, because I need it too."

Jim Knight, *Founder and CEO, Instructional Coaching Group, USA*

"This book is a powerful reminder that school leadership isn't about having all the answers—it's about understanding the weight of our influence and using it with intention, empathy, and clarity."

Peter DeWitt, *CEO, Founder, Facilitator and Coach, Instructional Leadership Collective, USA*

"Tamera Musiowsky-Borneman and C.Y. Arnold begin by looking at our human needs, what we need to be inspired, refreshed, and effective. They offer a refreshing and insightful way to look at work – and life. Their 5R's "decluttering" approach flies against our ingrained patterns of same old, same old. It asks that we pause, reflect, and move forward with visions and strategies that will benefit us and everyone with whom we work and play. This mindset is incredibly relevant today. This book is a treat!"

Thomas Hoerr, *Scholar in Residence, University of Missouri-St. Louis, USA*

"Tamera Musiowsky-Borneman and C.Y. Arnold have created a practical resource for educational leaders who want to simplify and streamline their workflow. Designed for school leaders looking to refine structures and systems, this new addition to their minimalist resources provides actionable tips and strategies aligned with the 5R's framework. Their approach offers a clear path to decluttering communication, improving time management, and tackling to-do lists with intention. It's a must-read for anyone who wants to create more efficient, effective systems that make a measurable impact in the daily lives of educators."

Monica Burns, *Founder, ClassTechTips, USA*

"Teaching is a profession of excess, and it's not for the faint of heart. That's why Tamera Musiowsky-Borneman and C.Y. Arnold's book on bringing minimalism schoolwide shows you how to improve the priorities and purpose in your teaching practice through the magic of 'less.' This book challenged me to rethink my habits, strip away what wasn't serving my students or myself, and approach my teaching with renewed clarity and purpose. And while it will certainly transform your individual teaching practice, the concepts also offer valuable insights for improving schoolwide systems and structures. If you're ready to rediscover the joy and impact of teaching, this book is invaluable."

Dan Tricarico, *High School Teacher, Author, and CEO, The Zen Teacher, USA*

Your School Leadership Edit

A Minimalist Approach to Rethinking Your School Ecosystem

Tamera Musiowsky-Borneman
and C.Y. Arnold

NEW YORK AND LONDON

Designed cover image: © Getty Images

First published 2026
by Routledge
605 Third Avenue, New York, NY 10158

and by Routledge
4 Park Square, Milton Park, Abingdon, Oxon, OX14 4RN

Routledge is an imprint of the Taylor & Francis Group, an informa business

© 2026 Tamera Musiowsky-Borneman and C.Y. Arnold

The right of Tamera Musiowsky-Borneman and C.Y. Arnold to be identified as authors of this work has been asserted in accordance with sections 77 and 78 of the Copyright, Designs and Patents Act 1988.

All rights reserved. No part of this book may be reprinted or reproduced or utilised in any form or by any electronic, mechanical, or other means, now known or hereafter invented, including photocopying and recording, or in any information storage or retrieval system, without permission in writing from the publishers.

Trademark notice: Product or corporate names may be trademarks or registered trademarks, and are used only for identification and explanation without intent to infringe.

ISBN: 978-1-032-93618-5 (hbk)
ISBN: 978-1-032-93617-8 (pbk)
ISBN: 978-1-003-56672-4 (ebk)

DOI: 10.4324/9781003566724

Typeset in Warnock Pro
by KnowledgeWorks Global Ltd.

Access the Support Material: www.routledge.com/9781032936178

Contents

Meet the Authors   ix
Foreword: Leaders, You Are in the Spotlight   xi
Lindsay Prendergast

▶ Introduction   1

▶ Chapter 1: Creating a Mindset and Culture for a Leadership Edit   21

▶ Chapter 2: Editing Communication   41

▶ Chapter 3: Editing Expectations   63

▶ Chapter 4: Editing Educator Support   91

▶ Chapter 5: Editing Your Time Structures   117

▶ Chapter 6: Editing Family Participation   145

▶ Chapter 7: Remedy Your Well-Being   171

▶ Chapter 8: Concluding Thought for Moving into Action   191

Meet the Authors

▶ **Tamera (Tammy) Musiowsky-Borneman** is a long-time educator, instructional coach, and author, dedicated to helping teachers simplify their practice and focus on what matters most. She is the founder of Plan Z Education Services, and through coaching and workshops, she supports educators in building confidence, streamlining strategies, and creating student-centered classrooms. Tammy is a 2014 ASCD Emerging Leader, serves as the Executive Director of the Advancing Leaders Collaborative (ALC) and on the board of the Hawai'i Society for Educational Technology (HSTE). Tammy co-authored the 2021 book, *The Minimalist Teacher* (ASCD), with C.Y. Arnold, and co-hosts their *The Minimalist Educator Podcast*.

▶ **C.Y. (Christine) Arnold** is a teacher, coach, coordinator, and author with over two decades of educational experience across Australia, Japan, Singapore, Belgium, and the Netherlands. As co-author of *The Minimalist Teacher* and co-host of *The Minimalist Educator Podcast*, C.Y. Arnold helps educators cut through the clutter to focus on what truly matters in teaching and learning. This is the second book co-authored with Tamera Musiowsky-Borneman, continuing their shared commitment to intentional, student-centered education and educator well-being.

Foreword
Leaders, You Are in the Spotlight

This book will not tell you how to run your school, tell you what kind of leader you are, nor is it a book with all the answers. It is a book that will remind you, though, that leadership is tough and that leadership development is a lifelong journey. The skills needed to be an effective leader begin early in life. You may remember being chosen as a student leader in your class or in your extracurriculars, and noted to be a student with "great leadership potential." And, as a teacher you probably remember the students in your classes that you relied on in the same way.

Leadership in schools is personified in several roles within our school community. We may see students speaking up to advocate for something they want or need. We may hear teachers sharing incidentally with each other to improve their practice. We may witness parents fundraising for a new tool or field trip to enrich the experiences of their children. Leadership can shine through from many different participants in the way they model behaviors to those around them in various capacities. What we know to be key here is that we can all influence others in the way we communicate, show up for our priorities, make use of our time, how we involve all community members in our work, and contribute to the culture of different groups we belong to.

We also know that there are those brave souls in our school buildings who take on the defined roles of leadership as we know them. Those who have raised their hand to venture into the driver's seat by helping others and by navigating the direct course of a school forward. Taking on this role can be a more cluttered and complex task than one could have imagined, and is likely to be far more than what is listed in your job description.

Taking on these leadership roles cannot be done lightly. The quality of our school leadership has a significant impact on school organization, culture, and the teachers in the building (Day et al., 2020). Subsequently, the teaching and learning environment can vary greatly depending on the success of the leadership, as can student achievement. Awareness of the significance of leadership roles is vital in order to have a positive influence.

The very nature of the job title you hold can be a huge impetus for impact. Robert Sutton (2010) coined the phrase "executive magnification," meaning that what you do and say is given far more weight, solely because the leader is saying it. He gives examples of off-handed comments being taken as mandates, simply because the "boss" made the comment. This kind of magnification can be seen in many different facets of our work in school leadership. The timing and tone of your email communication lets others know the boundaries of how they can communicate with their colleagues. Public praise of staff members lets others know what is desired and not desired. Choosing one teacher over another to host an observer in their room highlights whose practice is considered worthy. How you interact with and involve students models expectations for others. When and where do you take lunch and coffee breaks? Your attendance at school community events. Which parents are asked to help out? Each decision, interaction, and behavior may carry more weight, simply due to your job title. Others are looking to you for a model on how to conduct themselves within their working environment. If we are aware of the magnitude of how we show up at our schools, we can also imagine the consequences of carrying ourselves *without* integrity, thoughtfulness, empathy, and honesty.

Emotions can spread among groups of people as easily as the common cold. While emotions are not necessarily positive or negative, they can be perceived as such, and these emotions and emotional states have the capability of being passed back and forth around your school each and every day. In the field of Positive Psychology, this phenomenon is called emotional contagion and it has a very real impact on the experiences of people in organizations. If you are surrounded with people who feel happy, motivated, and engaged, you are more likely to feel that way yourself. In fact, positive emotions directly correlate to the self-reportage of job satisfaction and likelihood of retention (Williams et al., 2024). Unfortunately though, this can also be seen with the catching and spreading of what is perceived to be a negative emotional contagion in the workplace. To gain a wonderful insight into the reaching effects of emotional contagion and what you can do about it, watch Brandon Smith's (2016) TEDx talk on the subject.

Once more, we can see the amplified impact of the leaders' role. In her book, *The Art of Coaching Teams* (2016), Elena Aguilar reminds us that we can be instrumental in swaying the emotional tone in the building. "As the leader, your emotions matter the most …. You set the emotional standard" (p. 35). The difference between working for an employer who spends the day smiling and being uplifting, and one who scowls and finds fault, cannot be underestimated. Those in the community will look to you for the emotional cues of how to start and end the day, how to interact in all situations, and while facing challenges. The research into emotional contagion tells us clearly that you will probably receive back what you are sending out! With this thinking, we can connect these five ways to rethink what we do in our roles to the ideas that author Kutsyuruba shares with us in *Managing Today's Schools* (2022). This idea that leaders' well-being is entangled with the well-being of others as within a living ecosystem. Our own flourishing will benefit and support the collective flourishing.

Decision-making is another area of our work in leadership where our role magnifies what we do. The decisions we make can have far-reaching consequences and can literally make others' experiences at work more difficult or far easier. In other roles in schools, people's decisions may affect themselves, their students, and perhaps a small group of others. However, when in a leadership role, a decision has the power to lighten others' loads, engage people in the work they do, lift student growth, ensure systems run smoothly to support the work they do, increase productivity, and build joy. But the opposite can also be true, with our decisions ending up creating more work, more frustration, and disengagement from the people around us. Being mindful of the potential risks and rewards, and how all community members could be impacted, is important when making decisions. As is being timely about making decisions and being willing to return and reconsider decisions (Moore, 2022).

It is abundantly clear that school leadership is not a simple career swap or a few additional tasks to wrangle. Taking up the mantle also comes with the spotlight shining firmly upon you and the choices you are making each and every day. Working within leadership requires us to spend time reflecting on and exploring with honesty about who we are – our emotions, our personalities, our skill sets, and how culture has affected us (Aguilar, 2016). Intentional decisions need to be made in how we want to proceed and be perceived.

While the light may shine brightly upon you, there are many ways in which you can be rewarded in turn for the effort that you put out into your school community. As well as those extrinsic factors that may come to mind like the compensation package or status, there are many other sources of interest, motivation, and joy that come along with the work. The interpersonal relationships developed, seeing the achievement of your plans and goals, the responsibility and autonomy of the role, the opportunities to learn and grow, not to mention working alongside and for the benefit of the students: these are all sources of motivation to keep you going each day (Gacherieu, 2024). Principals often report having variety and interest in their work, with higher reports of job satisfaction (Kelly, 2023). Knowing that you have had a very real and tangible effect on your community is a takeaway from work that too few in society actually get to experience. You will not be counted among those who work away at a job, not ever really understanding the purpose of it all. The difference you make will be clearly seen around you, in the educational experiences of the students from year to year, the engagement and enjoyment of the school by the parents and the outcomes for the learning community of staff.

Through the dense thickets of how to effectively lead a school and its community, Maxwell, author of *The 21 Irrefutable Laws of Leadership* (2007), brings us back to our minimalist roots. "The true measure of leadership is influence. Nothing more, nothing less (p. 11)." If we thoughtfully carry this idea with us throughout our day, we can do our best work. While other tasks, complications, and barriers may take our attention, at the end of the day, leadership equates to influence. And what we do with this influence is up to us. As Uncle Ben tells a young Spiderman all the way back in 1962, "With great power there must also come - great responsibility!" (Lee & Ditko, 1962).

In the upcoming chapters, we will bring you to a place of rethinking what you can do to make things easier, more efficient, and maybe not clutter-free, but let's say, edited and clutter-reduced in your role and in the learning environment as a whole. If we can **reimagine** and **refine** what leadership means in our school community, we can transform the work that we do. **Reinvesting** in the key resource of schools, the people, helps us to work strategically toward our goals. When we **remove** unnecessary barriers to our work we can proceed with clarity and **repurpose** the skills and tools we already have to move forward with purpose. Our hope is that you take the time in the spotlight to share how you can create a place decluttered of the "unnecessities" (Musiowsky-Borneman & Arnold, 2021, p. 36) and shine the light on all the excellence and mastery your staff and students enact everyday.

▶ TRAITS OF A LEADER WHO VALUES LEADERSHIP EDITING

You are an educational leader who values a minimalist approach to leadership and that means you exemplify certain qualities and traits. These leaders work strategically to move the school culture and community to a place of wellness, trust, and responsibility by learning about what pockets can be emptied, rather than filled with more mysterious finds (Table F.1).

We know that you hold these traits and seek to embody these behaviors and actions because you are reading this book. If we are serious about changing how we do schools, it is also our responsibility to use these traits and be active with these behaviors so we can lead the change of what school is and what education looks like on a larger scale. Below, former school administrator, Lindsay Prendergast, Ed.D., reflects on her experiences and how she engaged in leadership editing by repurposing and refining some practices to open spaces allowing staff to focus more on their priorities.

Table F.1 Traits, Qualities, and Actions of Leaders Who Value Leadership Editing

Trait	Quality	Actions	What This Means to Your Community
Prioritizer	Discernment: Focuses on the essential tasks that align with the school's vision and goals, avoiding unnecessary initiatives that dilute impact.	Streamlines programs and projects to concentrate resources on what truly matters for student and teacher success.	School community members see your values in action.
Clear	Precision: Communicates goals and expectations succinctly and transparently, ensuring all constituents understand the direction.	Eliminates jargon and overly complex procedures, fostering a culture of simplicity and focus.	Trust is built through transparency and shared understanding.
Delegator	Empowerment: Empowers team members to take ownership of responsibilities, trusting their expertise and reducing micromanagement.	Builds collaborative teams to share the workload and decentralizes decision-making for efficiency.	Community members feel autonomous and invested in the work that is being done.
Mindful	Awareness: Cultivates awareness of time, energy, and resources, avoiding overcommitment and focusing on well-being.	Models self-care and encourages practices that support work-life balance among staff and students.	Well-being of all community members is enhanced, resulting in positive outcomes for all.

(Continued)

Table F.1 Traits, Qualities, and Actions of Leaders Who Value Leadership Editing *(Continued)*

Trait	Quality	Actions	What This Means to Your Community
Innovator	Creativity: Embraces creative solutions that achieve maximum results with minimal effort or resources.	Implements technologies and strategies that streamline workflows, such as simplified reporting systems or efficient meeting structures.	Inefficient working patterns are reduced, allowing for more positive workflow and engagement.

▶ A FORMER SCHOOL LEADER'S RESPONSE TO THE FOREWARD

Stepping into the role of a school leader is a profound responsibility – one that extends far beyond administrative duties or policy implementation. It is an act of influence, a commitment to shaping an environment where students thrive, teachers feel valued, and the entire school community moves forward with clarity and purpose. Reading the foreword to *School Leadership Edit* resonates deeply with me, as it captures the essence of what I have come to understand about leadership over the years: it is not about doing more, but about doing what truly matters.

I remember early in my career as a principal, I was eager to tackle every challenge, implement every new initiative, and be available to everyone at all times. I thought that being involved in everything would make me an effective leader. Instead, I found myself overwhelmed, and worse, I realized that my team was beginning to mirror my exhaustion. That was my first real lesson in leadership magnification. The way I approached my work – rushed, reactive, constantly on the verge of burnout – was influencing my staff more than any policy or initiative ever could. That realization led me to shift my focus toward clarity, intentionality, and trust in my team.

Tammy and Christine (Tamera and C.Y.) provide a refreshing perspective for leaders who, like me, have felt the weight of complexity and clutter in their role. It reminds us that leadership is not about controlling every detail but about setting the emotional and cultural tone of the school. The concept of "executive magnification" is particularly powerful. I recall a time when I casually mentioned in a staff meeting that I was considering restructuring our faculty meetings to be more collaborative. By the next day, multiple teachers had already begun rethinking their team meetings, believing change was imminent. What I had intended as a thought experiment had been received as a directive. That experience taught me to be more mindful of my words and the unintended authority they carried.

Moreover, the idea of emotional contagion is one that school leaders cannot afford to ignore. When I made a conscious effort to start my mornings by greeting staff with positivity, acknowledging small wins, and modeling calmness even in stressful situations, I saw a shift. Teachers, in turn, began their classes with a similar energy, and students responded in kind. This cascading effect demonstrated that my leadership was not about telling people what to do but about showing them how we, as a community, could navigate challenges with grace and optimism.

School Leadership Edit offers a pathway for leaders who seek to declutter their role – not by neglecting responsibility but by refining their focus. It encourages us to let go of the unnecessary, to empower our teams, and to invest in what truly impacts student learning and well-being. This approach does not diminish leadership but rather amplifies its effectiveness. As we step into our roles with intention, we create schools where teachers and students alike feel seen, supported, and inspired. And ultimately, isn't that what leadership is all about?

Lindsay Prendergast, Ed.D., Assistant Director of Strategy & Development, The Danielson Group, Co-Author of *Habits of Resilient Educators: Strategies for Thriving During Times of Anxiety, Doubt and Constant Change* (Corwin, 2024) and *Habits of Resilient Leaders: Personal Practices That Drive Professional Impact* (Corwin, 2025).

References

Aguilar, E. (2016). *The art of coaching teams: Building resilient communities that transform schools*. Jossey-Bass.

Day, C., Sammons, P., & Gorgen, K. (2020). *Successful school leadership*. Education Development Trust. https://files.eric.ed.gov/fulltext/ED614324.pdf

Gacherieu, D. R. (2024, May/June). Why principals stay. *Leadership, The Association of California School Administrators*. https://leadership.acsa.org/why-principals-stay

Kelly, H. (2023). *School leaders matter: Preventing burnout, managing stress, and improving wellbeing*. Routledge.

Kutsyuruba, B. (2022). Leadership for flourishing: Positive approaches to relationship building. In J. Glanz (Ed.), *Managing today's schools: New skills for school leaders in the 21st century* (pp. 97–110). Rowman & Littlefield.

Lee, S., & Ditko, S. (1962). *Spider-man! Amazing fantasy* (Vol. 1, No. 15). Marvel Comics.

Maxwell, J. C. (2007). *The 21 irrefutable laws of leadership: Follow them and people will follow you* (10th Anniversary ed.). Thomas Nelson.

Moore, M. G. (2022, March 22). How to make great decisions, quickly. *Harvard Business Review*.

Musiowsky-Borneman, T., & Arnold, C. (2021). *The minimalist teacher*. ASCD.

Smith, B. (2016, April 4). *Are emotions contagious in the workplace?* [Video]. YouTube.

Sutton, R. I. (2010). Good boss, bad boss: How to be the best … and learn from the worst. *Business Plus*.

Williams, C. E., Thomas, J. S., Bennett, A. A., Banks, G. C., Toth, A., Dunn, A. M., McBride, A., & Gooty, J. (2024). The role of discrete emotions in job satisfaction: A meta-analysis. *Journal of Organizational Behavior, 45*(1), 97–116.

Introduction

Doing less.
Minimalism.
Prioritizing.
Editing.

These phrases encapsulate the work that we care most passionately about. We want educators globally to think about how they can edit their work: revise, simplify, and focus on the key elements of what they do. Editing is about cutting out the extraneous and getting to the most clear and poignant part of what it is you are attempting to convey.

Generally we would not associate these words and ideas with education. We knew that exploring ideas of strategically lessening the stressful demands in teaching and leading schools would create a flurry of questions from educators about the connections we were trying to make. Honest questions such as "How can we even begin to think about this?" and "How is such a thing possible?" have been asked. Our response has consistently been – yes, we can do this and it is possible. As we shared ideas through writing, workshops, and our podcast, "The Minimalist Educator Podcast," we caught some attention with our seemingly outlandish ideas. We hoped these different ways of thinking about teaching and leading schools would potentially shift some mindsets; that perhaps transforming teaching and learning by being more intentional would create space for educators to pause AND still create rich educational experiences for learners through having a prosperous and fulfilling career as an educator. Our ideas were resonating with educators. And this excited us.

▶ WHAT WE'VE BEEN LEARNING

In 2021, we began talking about this approach to education publicly with the release of *The Minimalist Teacher* and have since been talking more with many educational leaders on our podcast. Since then, we have encountered the three predicted groups and their anticipated thoughts when sharing experiences and research about decluttering our educational spaces and seeking to be more strategic about what we focus on in schools. Of those that have been speaking about this work, our predictions have been confirmed and research validated. Roger's Diffusion of Innovation, a theory that delineates folks into particular categories when new ways of thinking surface (Musiowsky-Borneman & Arnold, 2021, p. 63) showed up as predicted.

Group One: Naysayers

- They are the folks that shake their heads, and say "not possible," or "no way in he– can we apply principles of minimalism in education." They have shared a blatant rejection of the idea that teachers could possibly keep their work contained within their contract hours.

Group Two: Tell Me More

- This group asks, "What is minimalism? I don't know much about this idea. I need to know more." (Great! We can work with this.)

Group Three: Let's Do This!

- This group has gravitated toward this transformational idea about changing the way we do school. They are using the tools and sharing them with colleagues.

We hoped there would be a set of educators who would exclaim "YES!" This is what we need to make education better for us and our students. We are happy to have had many reach out to us from across the world.

To support our educators and leaders in schools, we have learned from other writers such as Peter DeWitt, Lindsay Prendergast, and Piper Lee-Nichols how our ideas complement each other and offer practical actions to move a school from feeling cluttered and scattered to feeling purposeful and calm (Table I.1).

Table I.1 Connecting Ideas from Books on Intentionality in Schools

Book	Ideas from the Book	How These Ideas Support Editing and Strategically Doing Less
The Minimalist Teacher (Musiowsky-Borneman & Arnold, 2021)	Focus on purpose Sort out priorities Streamline and pare down initiatives, practices, and implementations Do what you do, but do it better	Help focus planning process Streamline making decisions Prioritizing
De-Implementation (DeWitt, 2022)	Different types of de-implementation Eliminate low value initiatives	Thoughtfully applying what works for your context Focus on high value initiatives
Habits of Resilient Educators (Prendergast & Lee, 2024)	Clarify your why Use data to drive decisions Prioritize effectively Set goals	Clarity aids in focus Identify what is impactful, which means we can remove what does not work Goals and priorities are given the most time and attention

After a webinar with Los Angeles Unified School District teachers, a teacher asked this question: "What do we do with all the 'mandates' from administration which add to clutter and detract from helping students? How [do we] communicate [this] with principals?" (personal communication, 2022). This is a question we hear again and again from teachers, yet administrators that come to our sessions ask how they can get teachers to focus less on inconsequential tasks that do not make teaching better. Teachers and administrators are asking the same question from within their respective roles! Both parties have the same desire to meet a need. Consequently, we offer similar responses to both groups. Perhaps then, there is a need for clarity in communication and expectations?

The attestations and questions above are ones we continue to hear. They are clearly resounding from a place of real concern and stress for those in education. How can we begin to compartmentalize what we do in our careers so we can find this balance? Educating our students occupies so much mental space, and educators are seeking ways to reclaim their own space and time. How can we learn from calm, purpose, and creating sustainable communities from those that live it? In 2022, Italy and Denmark were ranked first and second in the world for real work-life balance, according to the Organisation for Economic Co-operation and Development (World Economic Forum, 2022). Three indicators that measure balance are:

- the amount of time spent and not spent at work;
- how many hours a day are spent at the workplace;
- and how much time people have to enjoy leisurely activities.

Only 3% of working Italians work more than 50 hours a week, yet in the United States, more than 10% of Americans work more than 50 hours. When we look toward Asian culture, the Japanese philosophy of Ikigai is focused on elements of finding purpose. Ikigai is said to have "evolved from the basic health and wellness principles of traditional Japanese medicine" (Gaines, 2020). It is known as one's purpose, or what one finds fulfillment and joy in. Further to this, it "does not typically refer only to one's *personal* purpose and fulfillment in life, without regard to others or society at large." Is education not a place in which we should be seeking and promoting fulfillment for oneself and for all (Figure I.1)?

These questions from readers and conversations we have had with workshop participants have led us to keep writing about applying principles from minimalism to a broader scale in education. Going beyond what individuals or groups of teachers can do on their own, but ways in which the systems and structures are created and maintained at the school level, and how we can collectively find ways to become more strategic. This got us thinking more strategically about how we

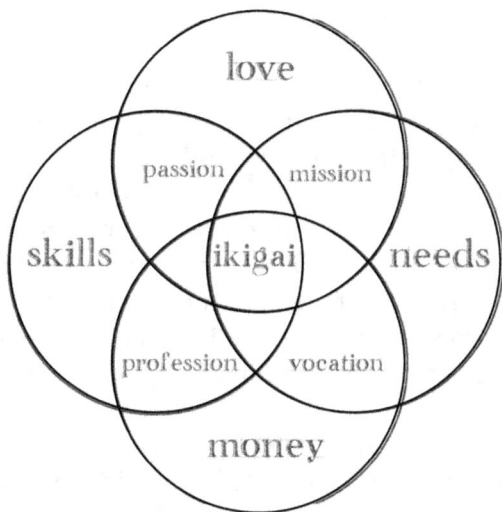

Figure I.1 Ikigai (The Japanese Secret to Joy)

Diagram of Ikigai, modified from Japan.gov (2022)

could learn not only to declutter, but to make edits to what we do to create a better and clarified school experience. Some question the feasibility, but we know it's possible with the right and ready mindset.

Educators who participate in our workshops have voiced the helpfulness of our version of an Eisenhower Matrix: the Urgent/important matrix (The Minimalist Teacher, p.27), for them in clarifying their priorities. It has assisted educators to reflect on their current lived experience within education, and where to direct their time and effort. Naomi Church, an educational consultant, told us she enlarged the matrix and used it with her family too (personal communication, 2021) (Table I.2).

Table I.2 Urgent/Important Matrix

	Urgent	*Not so Urgent*
Important	High priority: Take action immediately	Medium priority: Make a plan
Not so important	Medium priority: Make a plan	Neither urgent nor important: Eliminate as a priority

▶ FRAMEWORKS AS TOOLS

The beauty of writers offering frameworks, cycles, and flow charts is that they can be adapted to fit your context. You can use the tools, questions, and ideas offered, yet the purpose was for you also to be able to insert your own questions, ideas, and contexts as Naomi did. Intentionally decluttering and editing to lessen what you are doing in your school is not an initiative we are asking you to adopt. This is a purposeful thought and action process. One that requires all of us to question and reflect upon our practices, reimagining what school could – and should be.

This frequent cognitive work with educators constantly reminds us that we always need to be thinking about these ideas on a larger scale, so we started digging into and learning more about some school level systems and structures through experience, research, and interviews.

Between the two of us, we have been in education for almost 50 years and have held roles of educational assistant, classroom teacher, teacher team leader, school leadership team member, director of teaching and learning, coach, and more. In addition to this, we have experienced all kinds of systems: new systems, changing systems, efficient systems, and others ... not so much. We have also taught and led in public, independent, and international schools. As we started examining some larger school-based structures such as school expectations, teacher supports, and use of time, we knew we needed to deepen how we think about all the moving parts of a school environment. As a result of this experience, discussion, and to further our original frameworks, we are introducing the 5R's as a support for gaining depth in making cultural changes and adopting an editing culture in your school (Figure I.2).

What we mean when we are talking about the 5R's:

- Reimagine: When we evaluate the current vision and create a new one that more closely captures our purpose and priorities.
- Remove: When we subtract "unnecessities" such as redundant or excess information, expectations, resources, or materials.

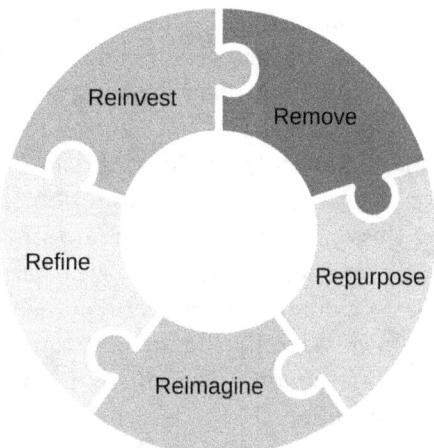

Figure I.2 The 5R's for Creating an Edited and Focused School Culture

- Repurpose: When we take what we currently have and create a new or better purpose for it.
- Reinvest: When we spend time digging in, learning more, and collaborating to achieve refined vision. We reinvest our time, money, and in people in order to meet our new goals.
- Refine: Reflect on and tweak your existing or new systems.

Since our first writings about bringing principles of "less is more" to schools in 2019, we have been reading literature and research, working with teachers and school leaders in the field across the world, and living out this approach in ways that make the most sense in our contexts. We hope our discussion of topics that have us thinking more about this thoughtful process of doing less, and better in our schools will spark some ideas and reflection for you too.

▶ HEURISTICS

Over the course of time, our brains have developed many thinking shortcuts to make faster, more efficient decisions and ways to solve problems with minimal mental effort. Once we have learned to do a task, we do not have to apply the same cognitive load to completing each task in the future. This frees up our brains to consider more challenging concepts, and of course, for our primitive brains, to ensure there are no lions about! The development of these shortcuts has been incredibly important for humans to develop the problem-solving and creative thinking skills we now use regularly.

However, these shortcuts in thinking can lead to various cognitive biases. Our brains make assumptions that they have seen a task like this one previously and jump straight into decision-making. But the decision chosen may be based on bias and error. These biases can force us to overlook relevant, pertinent information or to misidentify the actual reality of a situation. In *The Psychology of Stupidity: Explained by some of the world's smartest people*, Marmion (2020) describes that these cognitive biases can end up forcing otherwise intelligent folk to act or appear, well…. stupid! Concurrent to this idea, cognitive psychologist Yana Weinstein (2018) has a great analogy to explain the possible pitfall of heuristics. Weinstein describes heuristics like remembering the English spelling rule "i before e, except after c." This rule can help us make a quick decision in a lot of cases, but may end up steering us into error if we run into one of the many words that are exceptions.

In Table I.3, you will see a short description of a variety of cognitive biases and the ways in which this may be presented within a school environment.

So how does being aware of these cognitive biases assist us in our journey toward intentionally doing less? Often in schools, we make assumptions, perhaps in error, about the best way to proceed, why decisions have been made, how systems were developed, or the motivations behind people's actions. Which then leads us to back-tracking or wasted time and energy when we realize the dissonance between our assumption and the truth. Being aware of the biases our brains lean toward may help us slow down and pause before jumping to these conclusions and reduce the need to retract our responses. Plus, we think it's pretty awesome that our brains are hard-wired to be as efficient and as purposeful as possible!

Assistant Principal (AP) Cass has a few frequent visitors to her office because of disruptive classroom behavior. Because she sees Kyla at least three times a week for infractions, she makes an assumption that when she sees her huddled with a peer in the hallway, she is up to no good. AP Cass walks toward

Table I.3 Possible Points of Cognitive Biases in School Settings

Cognitive Bias	Description	Possible Example within a School Context
Availability heuristic	This heuristic helps us to think of how likely an event will occur, based on how quickly we can bring examples to mind.	Students assume that all group work projects will be challenging after one or two difficult experiences.
Representativeness heuristic	This heuristic helps sort things into likely categories, depending on how well we think they fit that category.	Assuming the outgoing, talkative student or teacher is going to be a clear, effective communicator.
Familiarity heuristic	This heuristic describes how we tend to favor activities or things that we are familiar with, rather than trying out something new.	Preferring to continue working with a known teaching approach, methodology, or resource, when something new may perhaps be a better choice.
Anchoring and adjustment heuristic	Overemphasis on one presented value when making judgments or estimates. Remembering an initial value and putting less importance on subsequent values.	Sticking with a plan based on initial assessment data and relying less on subsequent assessment data gathered.

Kyla and a peer, pointedly asks Kyla what she is up to, ignoring the student Kyla is interacting with. After several targeted questions about "what she is up to," Kyla cannot help but feel defensive and starts lashing back at AP Cass. Kyla tries explaining the scenario to her assistant principal but she gets sent to AP Cass's office, while the other student is sent on her way, leaving Kyla feeling even more downtrodden. When AP Cass arrives at her office, Kyla has calmed down, and is able to explain that she was helping her friend calm down after having experienced a domestic disturbance at home earlier that day. She further explains that she became so agitated by the accusations from AP Cass that she was having a hard time articulating what was happening with her. When AP Cass realizes she was in the wrong, she apologizes to Kyla and thanks her for supporting her peer. It was the availability heuristic at play that sent AP Cass into a pattern of assuming she knew the student's behavior because of past experiences. AP Cass's brain was working for efficiency, rather than with what the context actually was. How often has this happened with any of us in our roles?

▶ UNLEARNING AND RETHINKING

The knowledge we gain and understandings we develop about the world around us broaden and deepen over time. Consequently, the longer we live, the more potential unlearning and rethinking we must do. Unlearning requires us to create new and stronger neural pathways than the ones that currently exist. Society has influenced many to believe that "bigger is better." For example, fast food restaurants create bigger sizes and movie theaters try to upsell us a larger drink for just 50 cents more. Just because these options exist does not mean these are good ideas or that we cannot change our mind about them if we are trying to improve our health. It does make us rethink some of the societal ideas and habits we have created.

Dr. Adam Grant, organizational psychologist at the Wharton School in Philadelphia, writes about this shift in understanding and change in beliefs in his book *Think Again* (2021). Have you ever been told you are a "flip-flopper" or you change your mind too much? If you have, you are not alone. The good news here is that if you, in fact, changed your mind about something or had a shift in opinion, that means you learned something! Imagine that! Perhaps you once thought that the newest education trend on TikTok was just what you needed to get your students more engaged. But what you discovered was the preparation was too long and the payoff was limited, and so, you have learned that cutesy is not at all what you needed. You should take that learning as a valuable lesson next time you are scrolling to find new engagement ideas. What distinguishes a flip-flopper from someone who has changed their mind from learning something is the frequency of the mind-changing and how easily the mind gets changed based on what was learned. Now, what about if a new initiative is brought into your district and after a few months the district leaders change their mind because it is not meeting the needs of your constituents? Perhaps we can reframe this as a moment to rejoice rather than become frustrated by another change, and know that learning more can help us make better decisions. Abandoning a bad idea in the interest of student learning and removing another item from teacher plates is a call for celebration.

▶ RETHINKING THE MONEY SPEND

Have you worked in a school where all the walls are filled with posts, student work, quotes, and all the things? Have you been to schools that have all the EdTech gadgets? Multiple sets of manipulatives? New furniture? We have too. We know that sometimes these items serve a strong purpose. However, just because the walls are full, this does not mean all those things add value to the school's vision or physical environment. Just because you have the latest furniture for flexible seating, does not mean the furniture is used effectively for learning and meeting the needs of students.

When we have time to carefully plan budgets, ask teachers and students for feedback, we will realize that budgets can probably be spent more on people resources to support the staff in the school, rather than on things to fill the space. Perhaps we need to rethink and unlearn how school budgets are allocated and spent to ensure funds are distributed and spent with thought and more foresight, rather than, "hurry we have to spend this money by October 31st on xyz (even though we probably do not need them)."

At the beginning of the 20th century, school was a place in which goals may be viewed slightly differently than they are now.

American schools were viewed as places for children to learn about and preserve democracy, learn to "understand political and social issues and would participate in civic life, vote wisely, protect their rights and freedoms, and resist tyrants and demagogues. Character and virtue were also considered essential to good citizenship, and education was seen as a means to provide moral instruction and build character" (Kober, 2020). The purpose seemed to be clear.

Each decade, new initiatives and demands were built into the education system, often creating distractions from the intended purpose of education. The list has gotten longer and longer and educators have become more exhausted and spread thin. With a shift in the era of testing and the focus on college-preparation, it became part of our natural education process to overextend what students need to know resulting in adding more to the pile of content teachers are expected to "deliver." How can we begin to unlearn this idea that stacking content on our learners is beneficial and that perhaps we can spend more time developing critical thinkers and solution-finders? These changes in structures, curriculum adoptions, and implementations are on a continuous cycle of money-spend. Perhaps we should be rethinking how this money for curriculum is spent.

During the development of industry, schools began to look and sound a lot like factories. Horace Mann adopted ideas from Prussia in the 19th century with the idea that to scale schools "the factory line was simply the most efficient way to scale production in general, and the analog factory-model classroom was the most sensible way to rapidly scale a system of schools" (Rose, 2012). While creating this kind of system to scale might seem efficient, we know that this is an inefficient system for meeting the needs of our diverse learners. Has our monetary investment in this system been profitable?

▶ PARADIGM SHIFTS

There are certainly some historical ideas that we can back away from, yet there are also some that we might have to reinvest our time and money in because we know they are effective. Remember the one-room schoolhouse when children were placed in multi-age groupings? Research by Soliman and Okba (2006) support that multi-age and diverse groupings are effective for learning because they offer embedded opportunities for learner's thinking to be challenged, and is "not just limited to academic skills, but broadly engages each child's intellect, intelligences, interests, and understandings of morality" (DeVries & Zan, 2012; Katz, 2015). Yet, "the multiage, multigrade, single-room schoolhouse had virtually disappeared at the start of the 20th century but still existed in a number of small rural districts" (Lynch, 2020). "In 1910, a different structure for schooling was introduced, based on a six–three–three system" – the system most of us know today. Think about this. The structure of school widely used across the world is over 110 years old. Is it effective? Does it allow us to serve our purpose of educating well-rounded individuals and meet our educational priorities? Has it helped us spend our budgets in meaningful ways?

We have been shifting back to some of these initial approaches to education in recent years, and our experience trying to do school during a global pandemic seemed to accelerate some of these approaches. More and more schools are attempting to refocus on their learners and their school experience. Craig Schieber (2018) shares Paradigm shift: Learner-centered paradigm & networked age, written by Justin McKean, showing a distinct and meaningful paradigm shift in how we view and do school (Table I.4).

It seems as though McKean's ideas of education are ones that we see more and more often in educational magazines and as the topic in books. Why? Because they meet the purpose of education, which is not so different from the original goal – for learners to understand the world they live in. Why does it seem to be in our nature to overcomplicate our systems and implement changes that do not need to be made?

Klotz (2021) tells us about fascinating evidence that humans do indeed have a predilection toward adding, rather than subtracting. He outlines that people are driven to want to add things culturally, biologically, and economically, as well as just often omitting opportunities to see where subtraction could be helpful. It turns out, we are hardwired to want to add more, and have to be very mindful and deliberate in order to do less. What we really need to do is unlearn and rethink a lot of procedures

Table I.4 Justin McKean's Paradigm Shift: Learner-Centered Paradigm & Networked Age

Aspect	Current Paradigm	Learner-Centered Paradigm
World View	**Industrial Age**	**Networked Age**
Frame of reference	Factories and assembly lines	Networks and lateral connections
Model	School-centric: All systems are designed for efficiency in the delivery of standardized education	Learner-centric: All components are designed for an adaptable learner experience
Model components	Standardized age groupings Linear curriculum divided into subjects Purpose is to impact knowledge	Competency-based, personalized learning experiences Learning experiences enable the building of knowledge, development of skills and dispositions Embedded in stable, connected networks where relationships are prioritized

Source: Cited and Modified from Schieber

and structures if we want to do strategically less despite this historical and biological advancement toward more.

▶ NEEDS AND WANTS

Do you remember teaching the concept of needs and wants to your students or your kids at home? Sometimes not having our desires met can be a hard pill to swallow. We can feel emotional in these instances. It is a necessity to understand the difference between OUR needs and wants as educators. We can confuse what we need and what we want, and additionally think that what we want will benefit our students. We have listed a few things that people may think we need in schools:

- Lots of initiatives.
- All the teaching guides.
- Every kind of technology.
- Packed spaces.
- Behavior charts.
- External reward systems.
- Pretty bulletin boards.

When you were in your K-12 school years, who asked you what you needed in order to be a successful learner? Do you remember asking your students or staff? Was the response ever on that list above?

Let's rethink this. Here's what schools actually need:

- Curious learners.
- Qualified, thriving, and passionate teachers whose vision matches the school's.
- Appropriate size and strategic use of space.
- Intentionally chosen learning resources.
- Efficient and streamlined structures.
- Effective school leaders.
- Positive school climate and culture.

With this list in mind, we can reconsider our thinking on developing our schools with the systems and structures that will support prosperity in learning, for everyone, without clouding our decisions with our wants.

With all of this big picture discussion now laid in front of us, we can preview what each chapter in the book looks like.

▶ WHAT YOU'LL FIND IN EACH CHAPTER

In this *Introduction* chapter, we wanted to start you off with a dose of some of the ideas that will come up in different chapters. We introduced frameworks about minimalism and their possibilities in education, and a foundation of how we believe we can reframe our thinking about school cultures and ecosystems using our 5R framework.

Each chapter following this one has a similar flow, with some variation depending on the topic. You will notice that each chapter begins with a short introduction and then gives a summary of the 5R's for that element of school culture. This is to give you a quick snapshot of some of the specific strategies you will read later in the chapter. Following the 5R's summary, you will dig into some discussions which include some of the problems and concerns we encounter in schools about that topic. After this discussion, we share some research and considerations for you to think through as you begin your strategic processes of editing your leadership role. We wrap up each chapter with the discussion about the 5R's strategies and some lingering questions for you to consider for your work ahead. You will also notice that some ideas crossover chapters. For example, we discuss school accreditation processes and budgets in different chapters, yet with different lenses and for different purposes. Many of the intricacies of school culture and development tie into each other. It is hard to discuss expectations without also discussing communication. Watch for these threads throughout the chapters if you choose to read the book as a whole, and see how your vision of bringing principles of minimalism can shift these large-scale structures and processes in your school.

In *Chapter 1: Creating a Mindset and Culture for a Leadership Edit,* we discuss ideas about the importance of building trust and relationships and creating this as a centerpiece of your school's culture and ecosystem.

In *Chapter 2: Editing Communication*, we share the frustrations that stem from unclear communication and introduce use of the 5R's in your communication plans. Tools we provide can be used to support you in ensuring that you are effectively communicating with your school community members.

In *Chapter 3: Editing Expectations*, we focus on the development and implementation of strategic plans and other school expectations such as goal setting. We ask you to use the 5R's to create expectations and clear plans effectively and with purpose.

In *Chapter 4: Editing Educator Support*, we focus on the processes such as mentoring, coaching, observation cycles, and evaluations that are meant to support teachers in improving practice. We focus on the 5R's in the roles and relationships context to create a more effective teacher support system.

In *Chapter 5: Editing Your Time Structures*, we seek to provide some comfort to those of us who have felt the burden "not enough time." We dive into the construct of time and how to use the 5R's when planning and managing our time, and how to remove distractions.

In *Chapter 6: Editing Family Participation*, we consider how families and their engagement with the school community are vital for a strong community, yet attempts to develop a good relationship with families can fail. Here we are using the 5R's to look at engagement by placing value on diversity, and consider ideas for removing barriers to authentic engagement.

In *Chapter 7: Remedy Your Well-Being*, we acknowledge realities of the challenges of our work and highlight where we want all leaders to be. A place where leaders feel valued, productive, and clear-minded about the work they do through an understanding of well-being as an educational leader.

In *Chapter 8: Concluding Thought for Moving into Action*, we want to bring you to a place where you are ready to advocate and take action with the ideas you have read about, although you do not need to wait to read the concluding chapter to begin your decluttering process.

The 5R's provide an opportunity for authentic transformation to take place in your school structures. If you are reading this book, you are ready for this movement toward making your school ecosystem a more efficient place, allowing for a greater focus on teaching and learning, and more importantly, students and staff.

▶ WHEN AND HOW TO USE THIS BOOK

With the ideas we have presented in mind, we have a few suggestions for how you can move forward when reading this book.

We suggest reading the Foreward, Introduction, and Chapter 1 first and in order, whatever your role. This will set the stage for moving forward with a mindset of decluttering and refining your role so you can work with even more efficiency and focus. From here we suggest that you use the Urgent/important matrix to determine your highest priorities currently in your context in the Introduction Chapter. You will prioritize:

- creating the culture.
- defining your ecosystem.
- editing communication.
- editing expectations.
- editing teacher support systems.
- editing time structures.
- editing family participation.
- remedying your well-being practices.
- advocating for this mindset shift and culture change.

We know that priorities shift throughout the school year, so you will need to determine what is in front of mind for you at this moment in time, as you are reading this book.

You may also choose to read the book as a whole, which will give you a comprehensive look at bringing in principles and theories of minimalism and doing less better into your school. If you choose this method, revisit the chapter or chapters that speak to you most with your staff. You may want to choose one or two chapters for the entire school year to work through in PLCs or as a year-long book club. Whatever your choice, we are happy you are here with us on this journey to become more strategic about the aspects of your role as an educational leader so that your school culture feels more aligned with your vision and values.

Let's get started.

References

DeVries, R., & Zan, B. (2012). *Moral classrooms, moral children: Creating a constructivist atmosphere in early education* (2nd ed.). Teachers College Press.

DeWitt, P. M. (2022). *Deimplementation: Creating the space to focus on what works.* Corwin Press.

Gaines, J. (2020). *The philosophy of Ikigai: 3 examples about finding purpose.* Positive Psychology. https://positivepsychology.com/ikigai/

Grant, A. (2021). *Think again: The power of knowing what you don't know.* Viking.

Japan.gov. (2022). *Ikigai: The Japanese secret to a joyful life.* https://www.japan.go.jp/kizuna/2022/03/ikigai_japanese_secret_to_a_joyful_life.html

Katz, L. G. (2015). *Lively minds: Distinctions between academic versus intellectual goals for young children.* Defending the Early Years.

Klotz, L. (2021). *Subtract: The untapped science of less.* Flatiron Books.

Kober, N. (2020). *History and evolution of public education in the United States.* Center on Education Policy.

Lynch, M. (2020). *How the 20th century changed American education.* The Advocate. https://www.theedadvocate.org/20th-century-changed-american-education/

Marmion, J. F. (2020). *The psychology of stupidity: Explained by some of the world's smartest people.* Pan.

Musiowsky-Borneman, T., & Arnold, C. (2021). *The minimalist teacher.* ASCD.

Organisation for Economic Co-operation and Development (OECD). (n.d.). *Education policy review: Reviews of national policies for education.* OECD GPS. Retrieved October 10, 2024, from https://gpseducation.oecd.org/revieweducationpolicies/#!node=41732&filter=all

Prendergast, L., & Lee, P. (2024). *Habits of resilient educators: Strategies for thriving during times of anxiety, doubt, and constant change.* Corwin.

Rose, J. (2012, May 9). The factory line was simply the most efficient way to scale production in general, and the analog factory-model classroom was the most sensible way to rapidly scale a system of schools. *The Atlantic.*

Schieber, C. (2018, January 16). *We are in the midst of a historic paradigm shift in education.* https://aurora-institute.org/cw_post/we-are-in-the-midst-of-a-historic-paradigm-shift-in-education/

Soliman, M. H., & Okba, E. M. (2006). Teamwork as a New Sustainable Pedagogy for Teaching Architectural Design. Ain Shams University International Conference, Cairo, September 11–16, 2006, 181–192.

Weinstein, Y. (2018). *The availability heuristic*. The Learning Scientists. https://www.learningscientists.org/blog/2018/3/16-1

World Economic Forum. (2022). *These countries have the best work-life balance*. https://www.weforum.org/agenda/2022/05/the-countries-with-the-best-work-life-balance/

Chapter 1

Creating a Mindset and Culture for a Leadership Edit

Creating and growing a strong and sustainable school ecosystem requires intentional decision-making and a commitment to doing less, but better. By strategically applying ideas from the 5R's, school leaders can streamline their efforts while fostering a more cohesive and effective ecosystem. This approach begins by reimagining leadership through trust and relationship-building. It involves removing barriers that prevent meaningful collaboration and connection. Leaders can repurpose obstacles into opportunities for growth, while also reinvesting in key improvement processes. And, by refining the school's core values and purpose, leaders ensure that everyone's mission is aligned and all are working toward a shared vision of success. With this strategic editing process of revision and refinement, these elements of school culture will strengthen teaching and learning in your school. The summary of strategies in Table 1.1 will come up later in the chapter to support the development of your school's ecosystem. By creating effective structures and coming together with a common understanding, we can work toward doing less, better.

▶ CHANGING MINDSETS TO CHANGE OUR SCHOOLS

Working toward a minimalist vision of schools is a shift from our current one in education. Before we can make meaningful and sustainable changes in schools, we must work through changes in mindsets and behaviors first. Part of this mindset

Table 1.1 Summary of the 5R's in School Ecosystem Development

5R's	School Ecosystem Development
Reimagine	Leveraging relationships and trust development
Remove	Barriers from teachers so they can collaborate and build relationships
Repurpose	Goal setting and professional development to work toward shared goals
	Complaints and obstacles into opportunities for growth
Reinvest	In improvement plans and accreditation processes
Refine	Core value and purpose so all are on board

development means spending time developing strong cultures of respect, rethinking what we consider urgent, and recognizing that we can *all* take action. Educators are continually on the lookout for areas to improve and develop. But sometimes this can lead to overly focus on problem areas. Almost as if we are primed to identify issues, we are on guard for where we are not doing enough or where we are in deficit. It seems as though we are continually "getting caught in the loop of negative thinking" (Jha, 2020, p. 61) and rarely focus on what we might actually be doing well. We keep ourselves in a perpetual cycle of identifying and then "fixing" problems. There are gaps in learning and questions about who we are serving authentically. We are fighting for support, resources, and time. We battle social commentary on education and advice from all manner of voices. When one attempt has not worked the way we want it to, we replace it with something else instead. But at some point, we need to stop and question what we are in fact fixing, and whether we are doing it effectively. Those of us in education do so much already. Consider for a moment, what it could be like if there was time to develop our visions, mindsets, and relationships in a genuine way.

- Would making decisions be easier?
- Would we feel more productive?
- What if we had time to work through the communications, improvement plans, and expectations to become more efficient, less complicated, and more useful because you lived in a culture of mutual trust?

Reflect on these ideas as you begin to suggest or develop a culture in which everyone wants to be part of a more effective system.

▶ THE PROBLEM

This scenario may sound familiar to you. You start working on something and then realize you need something from another room. Upon reaching the other room, you have forgotten what it was you went in to retrieve. You stand there in confusion wondering what it was, and perhaps also what is wrong with your memory! You may do this at home as well as in your role at school – and this is a repeated occurrence. Why does this "Doorway Effect" happen to us? When our brains are busy, our working memory is overloaded. When we move to a different environment our brains are in a more vulnerable state, likely to forget what it was doing (Nield, 2021). Conversely, when our brains are left to focus on just one task, it is more likely that we can keep that idea at the front of our minds and not lose track of what we are doing. Our brains compartmentalize things as we think on them and are far better at doing it when we are not trying to do too much.

Why do we bring this up here? Because an educator's brain is overloaded. Educators continuously intake extensive amounts of information about processes, policies, and procedures. We need to know our students and staff, their needs, and how they are progressing. At all times we are mentally consulting schedules, curriculum documents, and to-do lists. If we have too many responsibilities, we are not allowing the brain to compartmentalize information efficiently. Operating within inefficient systems, or not allowing our brains the space they need to become attentive and focused can prevent us from reflecting and thinking critically. This may impact how we teach our learners and lead our staff.

In addition to the damage we are doing to creating environments where educators have the mental bandwidth to think critically and effectively, the constant state of overwhelm is having an impact on our well-being and health. Being constantly busy has an impact on the health of our relationships and our physical and emotional states (Clarke, 2022). In this way, educators are at higher risk of elevated feelings of stress, anxiety, sadness, loneliness, and anger. They are more likely to experience muscle tension, insomnia, and compromised immune and digestion functioning. Teaching was found to be one of the most stressful jobs in the United States, impacting teachers' mental and physical health, as well as student outcomes (Greenberg et al., 2016). And that was found even *before* the 2019 pandemic. School leaders are not immune either, similarly reporting elevated rates of stress, burnout, and protracted work weeks (Australian Institute for Teaching and School Leadership, n.d.). Wellbeing is an unavoidable element of an educator's life and so we dedicated a chapter later in the book on strategies to support you.

This physical and emotional toll has financial repercussions as schools battle with absenteeism and the cost of turnover. If, in addition to this, we add costs for programs, resources, and professional development that do not hit the mark, there is the possibility we will also diminish the budgets we need to work within. If it was feasible to work in an environment where we could all take stock, consider thoughtfully and prioritize, we may have the opportunity to positively shift our school cultures and entire ecosystems.

▶ ENACTING THE CHANGE

Finding time and space to recenter on purpose and sort through priorities is a process that can benefit an entire school community. Here's why.

You do not want to stay on auto-pilot and continue doing what you have always done. You are seeking *transformational change* for your school and community. Transformational change occurs by sharing the vision you are working toward, understanding the philosophy behind it, the approach, and benefits. Creating a shared understanding with all school community members allows for a culture of intentionality and strategic thinking to develop authentically. Having a shared vision, common language, and idea of how the future will look different from the past facilitates the change that needs to occur. It is only through establishing and communicating this shared vision that you can "go beyond 'stopping resistance' to creat(e) more and more people who want to help you" (Kotter & Rathgeber 2017).

For change to occur at an organizational or system level, there needs to be a pressing need to motivate this shift. In his book, *A Sense of Urgency* (2008), author and Professor of Leadership Emeritus at Harvard Business School, John P. Kotter, states that sometimes a sense of urgency comes from a crisis, which we believe feels all too familiar in our educational system. At times, we mistakenly look for quick ways to "fix" problems. We could shift our approach by removing clutter from our systems to focus on what truly is urgent. Yes, we want our students to become better readers, or to develop their social skills, but what might we lose in our rush to do so? A new initiative or program has the possibility to cause an increased sense of urgency. Is this urgency based on our real priorities, or is this perhaps a false urgency? "False urgency is almost always a product of failures or some sort of intense pressure that is put on a group" (p. 24). This intense pressure and failings could be produced, and felt by, any groups in our school communities. Those under false urgency feel anxious yet will undoubtedly take action. However, this action could end up being more activity-based, or forced, rather than productive and meaningful. Comparatively, operating with a true sense of urgency does not mean moving faster with less focus, it means the focus is clearer because you know what the real purpose is. With a clear focus on priorities, we can move the needle, and enact real change in our schools, for the benefit of all school community members.

This is a *focused* approach for creating an *intentional* culture of sustainable change. People who live by the principles of minimalism are focused on, and intentional about, each element of their lives. This creates a balanced approach to meet their purpose. This is the way to create sustainable practices and create longevity in their ecosystems. It is an investment in people; a culture of "we." We can create this focused and intentional culture by removing what is unnecessary and distracts from our greater purpose, which is educating future generations to be productive citizens with strong skill sets. In his book, *Focus: The Hidden Driver of Excellence* (2010), Daniel Goleman says that "[g]reat leaders do not settle for systems as they are, but see what they could become, and so work to transform them for the better, to benefit the widest circle" (p. 255). We are all leaders in the roles we hold in our schools and districts, so focusing on our purpose becomes the choice we all need to make.

Organizational Trust

One of the key indicators of an effective organization is that its members trust each other and feel trusted in return. To create strong cultures in schools, there must be a level of trust felt from and toward all participants. Without it, people may be reticent and not see the need to invest themselves in culture building. We choose not to use the term "buy-in" because we do not want people buying into anything, we want them to believe in the vision of creating a strong culture of trusted interactions. How do we build an ecosystem together by bringing in ideas from voluntary simplicity and minimalism ("reducing focus on accumulating material goods and wealth ... [while] increas[ing] focus on personal growth and values") (Hook et al., 2018, p. 131)? Or even the Japanese philosophy around Ikigai; principles we associate with finding balance in lifestyle and in life's purpose and apply them in education? We first build an understanding from research and also learn from the stories of those who live and find success in these principles and practices. This helps us build a level of trust that these practices are for the common good of those in our school communities.

Why Relationships Are the Key to Change

With strong and trusting relationships among school members, organizations can withstand obstacles and smoothly overcome barriers. In education, we sometimes apply band-aids and ointments to issues that occur, but those band-aids are not always the size or stickiness we need, nor do they prevent further damage from occurring. We could think about the ways we can develop solid foundations for our relationships, instead of putting band-aids on faulty ones, and skipping time investment to build and maintain them. We often engage in team-building activities at the start of a school year and at staff meetings. This is one way to build relationships, in a way that we can interact and view each other in a different light from everyday activity. However, we need opportunities to develop bonds of trust among our peers to build a strong culture. In a community where people trust each other to do what is best for the greater good, change has a place to happen. People open up. When people see how they can rely on each other, they become invested. Because there is trust, they feel good, and their levels of dopamine increase. In the long term, this investment in building relationships may prevent cracks in your foundation, which can damage your entire school culture, and student learning and success as a consequence.

Another understanding to justify why a focus on relationships is crucial in our school ecosystems is gender. Our schools are still predominantly favored as a place of occupation by those identifying as women. This is in step with all of the caregiving professions; working with children is still largely the domain of women. What influence does this have on the importance of developing relationships? There is evidence that finds that women are more likely to attach their feelings of self-esteem, self-worth, empowerment, and achievement to the success of their relationships (Guerrero et al., 2022; Mandal & Moroń, 2019; Surrey, 1985). While those identifying as men may attach their values of self-worth to competition, achievement, and standing, women often attach much of their self-esteem to how well their relationships are going. So the problem becomes clear if these heavily female workplaces are experiencing conflict, mistrust, or disconnection. Building cultures of trust founded in strong relationships will win us the added benefit of staff feeling that their self-worth is increased! If we aim to build organizational trust in order to positively alter our culture, it is imperative that we acknowledge the importance of successful relationships among those working there.

Habit Change: Shifting Culture

In the Introduction chapter, we mentioned our work with several groups of educators. Administrators have shared that they wish their teachers would be on board with a minimalist approach, and conversely, teachers have shared that they wish their administrators would dial down on the initiative add-ons and program changes. In these situations, relationships matter more than we realize. If the ideal goal from all constituents is to be more thoughtful and sustainable in our practices, who is responsible for starting the editing process?

Good news! Anyone can start in their own way. Anyone who can make decisions can choose to begin this journey. We would support the idea that someone choosing to start this journey of finding purpose and clarity understands the benefits of this process and outweighs any impending feelings of "why am I doing this?" This process is one that benefits not only the action-taker, but those in their circle, therefore positively impacting relationships.

A great place for anyone to start is to first consider their purpose, their priorities to meet this purpose, and then, what can be pared down in order to meet the purpose and priorities (Musiowsky-Borneman & Arnold, 2021). This simple three-step process allows practitioners to focus on where to place their efforts, time, and focus. As well as recognize that not all possible items on a task list are needed to feel great about the work you are doing (Table 1.2).

After establishing these individual stepping stones, we can examine how this process supports us in building culture in our school contexts. For example, Shondra, Vrita, Marty, and

Table 1.2 Finding the Purpose, Priorities, and What to Pare Down

Triple P	Example 1	Example 2	Example 3
Purpose	To find clarity in systems	To ensure student success	To remove extraneous tasks from teacher's responsibilities list
Priorities	To ensure expectations are met	To remove barriers to learning	To promote teacher well-being
Pare down	Few expectations are communicated at once and are impactful OR Communications are sent out with regularity and in concise terms	Learners feel safe in the environment OR Learners have access to materials and resources they need to learn	Streamline tasks within teams OR Build the timetable to allow for common planning time

Darnell work at the same school and all want to begin a streamlining process and become more efficient with tasks that get them bogged down, and free up some much-needed mental capacity. Shondra is an upper elementary classroom teacher who wants to think about her use of wall space and the use of display boards. Vrita is a principal and has made the decision they need to sift through their notes from their last administrator meeting to pull out priorities that align with the school improvement plan. Darnell is a support teacher and makes the conscious decision to put some of the supplies he has in his cabinets back in the resource room to save space for essential items. Marty is a primary teacher and is at the beginning stages of making some mindset shifts. He wants to know more about minimalism and how to use his classroom space in a more effective way. He sees the energy and engagement of his colleagues and their students in the organized classroom space, and wants to know more about how to do this. This start is just the first step in a change that Shondra, Vrita, Marty, and Darnell are choosing to make. Sharing their vision for reducing clutter and editing practices is a place to begin. This way they can understand each other's priorities while supporting their individuality and building trust within relationships during this process.

Here is how these individual entry points can begin the culture creation in one school when we examine what this can look like, sound like, and feel like (Table 1.3).

Shondra, Vrita, Marty, and Darnell agreed that knowing each other's goals helped keep them accountable and on track for keeping their priorities clear and met. Understanding their relationships helped them identify what they needed to do for each other during this process. While Darnell only needed an initial conversation to get his process started, Vrita required more time investment from their colleagues to support the consistency in always getting their administrator notes and communications in order for sharing. Shondra is already working on applying this mindset to the environment and is willing to support Marty as he begins his learning journey.

This work by Shondra, Vrita, Marty, and Darnell set the stage for collaboration in the school ecosystem. Although they are working in different roles and on different goals, they have each

Table 1.3 School-Based Examples

Who	Priority	How It Creates the Culture
Shondra, upper elementary classroom teacher	Reimagine the use of wall space in classroom	Shondra visibly shares that she values the use of space through her reimagination of wall space
Vrita, school administrator	Relay essential and plan-aligned information to staff from meetings	Vrita shows she values people's time and mental capacity
Darnell, support staff	Remove nonessential items from storage space	Darnell shows that he values only having essentials at hand, keeping extras out of sight until they are needed
Marty, primary teacher	Wants to learn about minimalism and adding value to his spaces	Marty's interest in minimalism aligns with what his colleague's actions

other for sounding boards. They can meet in their teams and share their successes about these transformations. Built on a foundation of trusting relationships, this is a starting point for collaboration on the editing process in their school.

THE 5R's: EDITING STRATEGIES FOR CREATING MINDSET AND CULTURE

We mentioned in the introductory chapter that we framed out the 5R's as a support for gaining depth in making ecosystem changes and adopting an "editing" approach in your school. As we begin to get into discussions and strategies for thinking through and living the 5R's in your school, we ask you to think very deliberately about the leadership you bring to your school, and how you play such a pivotal role in supporting the development of this culture.

▶ REIMAGINE

Relationships

To support ecosystem development, we often think about the important role relationships play. Without strong relationships and trust, it can become a challenge to make change. This is why understanding the dynamics or forces within and among relationships can help us make the changes we want to make. In *Forces of Influence: How to Leverage Relationships to Improve Practice* (2020), Fred Ende and Meghan Everette, Ed.D., discuss the four forces to leverage to build relationships: the pull, the push, the shove, and the nudge. A pull is a relationship that requires high initial involvement and high ongoing support. A push requires low initial involvement and high ongoing support. A shove requires low initial involvement and low ongoing support, and a nudge requires high initial involvement and low ongoing support. You could see these forces at work for Shondra, Vrita, Marty, and Darnell in the example above. Here is how we see these forces supporting you in moving forward to building a strong culture of minimalism in your school (Table 1.4).

Trust

We discussed above how important it is to build organizational trust, and that without trust among staff, cracks will appear in the foundation of our systems. But how do we go about building trust? There are many resources out there providing tips and ideas about the best way to build and improve trust in schools. Many of these resources offer helpful suggestions for staff to earn trust with others, such as communicate effectively, listen, share decision making, apologize when necessary, be authentic, and get to know others authentically (Waller, 2021). These are all important elements and needed advice for all of us when working in a collaborative setting. However, there is another consideration that is needed if we are in a leadership position within our schools. This is that we need to lead with and grant trust, rather than earn it over time as we would when working alongside others. "Leaders need to earn the trust and teammates need to earn each others' trust, but leaders earn trust by extending it. Great educational leaders trust in others before it's

Table 1.4 Four "Forces of Influence" in Relationships

Force	Who	How to Leverage This Force
Pull	Marty	Someone that is highly initially involved in supporting a colleague and will remain a support will be strong advocates of creating a culture shift and focus on purpose and priorities in your school in a sustainable way.
Push	Vrita	Someone who has low initial involvement in supporting a colleague, yet will be a consistent long-term support and a dependable advocate of creating a culture shift and focus on purpose and priorities in your school in a sustainable way.
Shove	Shondra	Someone who has low initial involvement in supporting a colleague and who has low ongoing support may be already invested in existing relationships, and therefore not require as much support because of the strength of current relationships. They already understand the importance of creating the culture together and can naturally keep the momentum going.
Nudge	Darnell	Someone who has high initial involvement in supporting a colleague and maintains a low level of ongoing support knows that the initial investment in the relationship is needed to create the culture, and also knows that the other party will not need as much support moving forward.

earned and only when it is broken do they take it away" (Jones et al., 2022). It is key that when in leadership roles, we recognize the different approach we need to take toward organizational trust in our workplaces. If we expect to slowly build trust in our staff over time, like we would when working alongside them, we are bound for conflict. Instead, we need to grant that trust upfront and seek to reinforce it with mutual trust through our actions over time.

▶ REMOVE

Barriers

We know that collaboration is a key, important element of a trusting school culture. Just as we want to remove barriers to student learning, when we have an expectation that teachers will collaborate with one another to create richer learning experiences for students, barriers to do so must be removed. Common barriers to collaboration include:

- rigid school schedules.
- too many tasks to tackle in planning periods.
- no common planning time.
- no agenda or vision for collaboration or collaborative projects.
- relationships in the team lack trust.

What might be the first barrier that can be addressed here? How can it be addressed? If teachers currently are without a common planning block, evaluate the timetable to find even small blocks of time that can make the schedule more collaboration-time friendly. Create clear expectations around how collaboration meetings will run, what the norms are, and how they are documented. Putting time, focus, and energy upfront and in the short term with items such as these may enable barriers to be removed and collaborative cultures to bloom.

▶ REPURPOSE

Goal-Setting

We will dig deeper into goal setting in the "Editing Expectations" chapter, yet we wanted to touch upon it in this section as we know that goal setting is a large part of creating a shared vision and building a strong school culture. When groups or individuals engage in goal setting, there are many different themes, topics, or pathways that could be focused on. What if we leveraged the goal setting cycle to aid in the development of our mindsets and school culture? What could we achieve in creating our goals around doing strategically less? And, no, we do not just mean writing ourselves a goal of *"do less."* As wonderful as that may be! When goal setting protocols are repurposed around strategically building a mindset and positive school culture, more of the work we want to do becomes clear and decluttered. Here are some goals to build cultures and mindsets:

- Being transparent in communication with students and staff.
- Build agency in students and staff by enlisting help with decision making.
- Communicate and celebrate successes.
- Model professional behavior in collaborative meetings.
- Use new protocols to develop mindsets.
- Use tools and strategies to prioritize collectively as a staff.

Complaints and Obstacles into Opportunities for Growth

Earlier in the chapter, we discussed the mindsets we have when working in school contexts. We want to fix things when concerns are raised or complaints are made, and we sometimes think with a deficit mindset. It seems that reverting to this way of thinking is most comfortable for us because it is what we have always done.

How easy is it to take a complaint, obstacle, or challenge and repurpose that into a productive thought, action, or opportunity for growth? It sounds easy, yet requires some slowing down to pause and strategically think. Expert business coach, Phil Dobson, leverages neuroscience and psychology to enhance individual and organizational effectiveness. He tells us that in order to reframe a problem and avoid jumping straight into solutions, we need to pause and pose questions that will aid you in finding the right solution (2021). Asking questions in order to reframe the problem allows us to be reflective and innovative, as well as build positivity through a growth mindset. Table 1.5 is a bank of examples showing how you can repurpose that negative into a positive through questioning:

The helpfulness of reframing obstacles into opportunities can not be underestimated when building transformational cultures and mindsets in schools. Asking questions in this way shifts our thinking into a more positive, glass-half-full, constructive perspective.

Table 1.5 Complaints and Opportunities for Growth

Complaint (Obstacle)	Opportunity for Growth
Teachers have another new initiative to learn	What prioritization exercise can we do to support teachers with this new information?
Communication is unclear	How can we audit our communication practices to best serve our community?
Excessive administration/ paperwork tasks	What administrative tasks do we have that have the highest impact on teaching and learning? What tasks have lower impact? How do we know?

▶ REINVEST

School Improvement Planning and Accreditation

Schools that undergo an accreditation process or a "grading" system that requires an audit of initiatives, protocols, procedures, programs, and other school-related functions sound like so much work. Taking time to go through school systems is an extremely valuable process to determine what works well, and what is not adding value. This process gives all constituents clarity on both where the school has come from, where it is currently and a vision of what the future could be. We have both been involved in school accreditation processes and we came away with several highlights (Table 1.6).

Notice a trend? Similarly, we can compare this to author Robyn Jackson's, school improvement cycle in her book, *Stop Leading, Start Building: Turn your school into a success story with the people and resources you already have* (2021). In her work, Jackson emphasizes that school leaders must shift from traditional leadership roles to "builders" who use the resources and people they have to achieve success. Jackson suggests that rather than creating the school's improvement plan at the start of the academic year and leaving it to bake for the year, school staff should revisit the improvement plan in 90-day cycles. The purpose of these shorter-term cycles is to see what is working and make revisions when needed and within the spaces

Table 1.6 Outcomes from School Accreditation Process

Learned About...	Found Out...	Why This Is Important
School governance	The entire decision-making chain of command, understanding of culture and history	Helps find purpose, reestablish priorities, and pare down unnecessary and irrelevant information, programs, etc.
School policies and procedures	The purpose of some policies and procedures; ensuring that you are utilizing this in your own practice	
Roles and responsibilities	Clarity around school structure and organization	
Documentation	Clarity in expectation, understanding purpose	
Communication practices	Clarity in process and expectations	
Programming	Clarity in student learning processes	

that require changes. We were fortunate to have school leaders when we taught together in Singapore that were always revisiting the purpose of the processes and professional learning in which we were participating. This leadership example of keeping our work intentional helped us stay focused.

Reimagining and reinvesting in school improvement cycles in this way opens an exciting entry point for schools to become intentional about the time and energy we spend on initiatives and programs. A 90-day cycle provides opportunities to review and reflect strategically to ensure everyone is maintaining their attention and pulling in the same direction.

In order to elevate the power of this shorter cycle, you could add a dimension of financial review into this 90-day round. Thus, increasing the probability that financial expenditures are going toward what the goals and intentions of the community are at any particular time. As mentioned earlier, school contexts can at times look for a quick fix, which means that our budgets may not be serving the needs of the community.

Ross (2015) reports that the states of New York and California are "home to some of the most wasteful K-12 spenders." As a recent notable example of this, the New York City Department of Education spent millions of dollars on a literacy program in the first two decades of the 2000s. Hundreds of schools spent considerable time and energy learning and delivering this city-wide mandated program, only to later uncover cognitive scientists' and education researchers' concerns that the approach does not take into full consideration the needs of all learners and best practice in promoting student learning (Cabell, 2022). While a 90-day cycle review may not have saved the millions, a priority and needs check-in with some feedback to the districts about the money spent could have saved teachers some frustration trying to teach a program that was not meant for millions of children who needed more than the program had to offer (Pondiscio, 2020).

Moving from a "get this to fix that" reactive spending mindset to one where our financial spending is closely aligned with our purpose and priorities will provide a greater educational experience for all constituents. We want student growth and learning, teachers enchanted with their profession, and administrators who can see the impact of their work. Aligning our review systems and budgets can only serve to bring us closer to these goals. In the chapter, "Editing Expectations," we will take an in-depth look at how the 5R's can look in your school development plan.

▶ REFINE

Values

Most educational institutions have some form of a mission, vision, or value statements. Ideally, these serve a purpose beyond lettering on the walls. These should be a statement of a common ideal that the community is striving toward. It should be a summary of the culture, the collective beliefs, and hopes for all school community members. But in order for this to be effective, these value statements must be known and understood by all (Mucinskas & Clark, 2022).

Having all staff participate in revisiting the school's values to refine the mission and vision is an essential exercise to ensure that in fact, all school staff and parents understand the values the school holds. In this case, the school community is strategically working toward less clutter and more high-value relationships, a common goal, and a trusting learning environment.

A rejuvenation of these year-long processes and goals offers multiple opportunities for thought and reflection. Could this be the place that would allow constituents to see where purposes and priorities lie and if it supports a streamlined and more efficient future? Once the culture of editing to strategically do less is created in a school, where everyone shares a vision of purpose and the necessity to edit process, structures, and systems, it is possible to work through the foundational layers of what can make a school successful through the 5R's.

LINGERING QUESTIONS

- How do the relationships I have with my colleagues influence the culture of our school?
- How does this influence our school ecosystem?
- How can we reimagine our ideas and actions so we can focus on purpose and value overall?
- How can we strategically reinvest time into our school's plan?
- To what extent are we living our school mission, vision, or values?

As we move into the next chapters, keep these culture building and ecosystem development pieces in mind. School ecosystems are complex and require intentionality in the building process. In Chapter 2, we are diving into the highly complex system of school communication. With the idea of keeping communication deliberate and focused, we will use the discussion sections of the chapter to build an understanding of the strategies highlighted in the 5R's section.

References

Australian Institute for Teaching and School Leadership. (n.d.). *Wellbeing in Australian schools.* https://www.aitsl.edu.au/research/spotlights/wellbeing-in-australian-schools

Cabell, D. W. (2022, August 23). Readers workshop is a science-denial curriculum. Thomas B. Fordham Institute. https://fordhaminstitute.org/national/commentary/readers-workshop-science-denial-curriculum

Clarke, J. (2022, May 23). *If you're always over-scheduled, find out why you need to slow down.* Verywell Mind. https://www.verywellmind.com/how-the-glorification-of-busyness-impacts-our-well-being-4175360

Ende, F., & Everette, M. (2020). *Forces of influence: How to leverage relationships to improve practice.* ASCD.

Goleman, D. (2010). *Focus: The hidden driver of excellence.* HarperCollins Publishers.

Greenberg, M. T., Abenavoli, R. M., & Brown, J. L. (2016, September 1). *Teacher stress and health.* RWJF. https://www.rwjf.org/en/insights/our-research/2016/07/teacher-stress-and-health.html

Guerrero, M., Longan, C., Cummings, C., Kassanits, J., Reilly, A., Stevens, E., & Jason, L. A. (2022). Women's friendships: A basis for individual-level resources and their connection to power and optimism. *The Humanistic Psychologist, 50*(3), 360–375. https://doi.org/10.1037/hum0000295

Hook, D., Jensen, C., Simms, T., & Waller, S. (2018). Pathways to sustainable living: Examining value shifts in modern society. *Journal of Sustainability Studies, 34*(2), 118–142.

Jackson, R. R. (2021). *Stop leading, start building: Turn your school into a success story with the people and resources you already have.* ASCD.

Jha, A. P. (2020). *Peak mind: Find your focus, own your attention, invest 12 minutes a day.* HarperOne.

Jones, J. M., Vari, T. J., & Hamilton, C. (2022). *7 mindshifts for school leaders: Finding new ways to think about old problems.* Corwin.

Kotter, J. P. (2008). *A sense of urgency.* Harvard Business Press.

Kotter, J. P., & Rathgeber, H. (2017). *Our iceberg is melting: Changing and succeeding under any conditions.* Penguin Random House.

Mandal, E., & Moroń, M. (2019). Contingencies of self-worth and global self-esteem among college women: The role of masculine and feminine traits endorsement. *Social Psychological Bulletin, 14*(3). https://doi.org/10.32872/spb.v14i1.33507

Mucinskas, D., & Clark, S. (2022, September 8). *How to make mission matter at your school.* Harvard Graduate School of Education.

Musiowsky-Borneman, T., & Arnold, C. (2021). *The minimalist teacher.* ASCD.

Nield, D. (2021). What did I come in here for? New study explains the weird "doorway effect." *Science Alert.* https://www.sciencealert.com/scientists-find-the-doorway-effect-could-be-real-but-only-in-overloaded-brains

Pondiscio, R. (2020, April 3). *At this time of crisis, schools are improvising, innovating and scaling good ideas with love, loyalty & care.* Thomas B. Fordham Institute. https://fordhaminstitute.org/national/commentary/lessons-last-time-pandemic

Ross, T. F. (2015, January 15). Where school dollars go to waste. *The Atlantic.* https://www.theatlantic.com/education/archive/2015/01/where-school-dollars-go-to-waste/384949/

Surrey, J. L. (1985). *Self-in-relation: A theory of women's development* (Work in Progress No. 13). Wellesley College, Stone Center for Developmental Services and Studies.

Waller, A. (2021, December 20). 6 simple ways to build trusting relationships with staff. *Edutopia.* https://www.edutopia.org/article/6-simple-ways-build-trusting-relationships-staff/

Chapter 2
Editing Communication

In the fast-paced world of school leadership, communication is at the heart of everything we do. Yet, too often, it becomes cluttered, overwhelming, and ineffective. That's why it is time to reimagine the purpose of all communication – focusing on clarity, connection, and impact. By embracing the following 5R's, school leaders can streamline communication, foster stronger relationships, and create a school culture where every message truly matters (Table 2.1).

Table 2.1 Summary of the 5R's for Decluttering and Editing Communication

5R's	Editing Strategies
Reimagine	The purpose of all communication
Remove	Barriers to communication
Repurpose	Your current communication systems
Reinvest	In your tools In your habits In expressing gratitude
Refine	What you have already been doing How you use your time

▶ COMMUNICATION, GENERALLY SPEAKING…

Communication is a highly complex structure in which all humans engage. Babies are born communicating their needs through cries and whimpers. Toddlers test language, communicating through babbling and tantrums, often leaving parents guessing what their children need or want. Children and teens communicate with more complex language and nonverbal cues while they gain experience, and in adulthood we have become master communicators, right? Not necessarily! Communication is challenging not only because it means someone is both receiving and expressing information and emotions, but also because there are multiple parties involved in the process. Let's be clear about who those "parties" are. Those "parties" are humans. People we work with every day. This is critical to remember when we encounter frustration and impatience. If we think of our message processes as "human-centered communication" (Beute & Puccinelli, 2021), we can realize that this "allows other people to feel seen, heard, understood, and appreciated" (pp. 203–204). Communication is about sending and receiving all kinds of messages.

▶ THE COMPLEX WEB OF SCHOOL COMMUNICATION

In a 2024 large-scale well-being–focused survey of teachers internationally, TES, an international education organization, found that only 22% of survey takers felt that there is a cohesive communication strategy in their workplace. This research highlights a significant need for a thoughtful approach to the communication taking place in our schools. Interestingly, the senior leader respondents reported that 72% of them have a voice in the running of their school and 60% feel that information is shared effectively at their school. These responses are markedly above the findings from middle leaders and teachers themselves. Is this a case of some sections of schools feeling like the messaging is clear, while others do not have the same perception? What checks and balances do we have in place to ensure that our messaging is seen and understood?

These scenarios may be familiar to you:

- As a school leader, you have to make a last-minute change to the school schedule because of something that has come up. You do not communicate this change in a timely manner to teachers and students. This leads to an expected outcome of confused and frustrated teachers.
- Or, your school has conducted parent-teacher conferences in the same way since the school opened 20 years ago, and teachers advocate to change the conference style to student-led conferences. Teachers thought you were going to communicate this change to parents, and you thought teachers were communicating the change. Parents schedule their times as usual, but when most parents arrive, they do not bring their child to lead the conferences, defeating the purpose of having student-led conferences.

What can you recognize within these scenarios? Are memories and emotions surfacing? How can we avoid these blunders in our lines of communication?

The communication structures and systems in schools are complex. Multiple lines of communication are simultaneously occurring, between and across multiple different groups of constituents. Managing and maintaining those lines of communication takes skill and know-how. Here is what those lines of communication can look like in schools:

- Administrator–Staff, and Staff–Administrator.
- Administrator–Parent, and Parent–Administrator.
- Administrator–Student, and Student–Administrator.
- Teacher–Parent, and Parent–Teacher.
- Teacher–Student, and Student–Teacher.
- Staff–Staff.
- Administrator–Staff–Parent and so on.

Educational institutions are social endeavors. They are, by nature, a space in which communication is a necessity. If our aim is to be integral to the efficient running and improvement of these institutions, not just temporary participants or outside observers, we must work towards being expert communicators. We need to be able to listen to understand, know our audience, get to our point quickly and clearly, predict resistance, and call others to action. Falling short of being a great communicator means we are adding to workloads and misunderstandings, whilst damaging culture, trust, and relationships.

Unfortunately as adults, sometimes we use methods of getting our messages out with clarity, and other times, our messages are confusing. While we may not think we are babbling or unclear, we may end conversations leaving others confused and questioning what the conversation was even about, or write emails leaving recipients with more questions than answers.

▶ COMMUNICATION STYLES

How does this confusion come about? When does communication become more difficult and more challenging, making it harder for us to get our message across to our intended audiences? Communication brings out who we are. When we communicate with others, we bring our communication styles, preferences, personalities, tones, and nuanced speech. It is no surprise that any of us might experience confusion or misunderstandings in communication. For effective and clear communication, it may be first important to understand that there are different communication styles.

Expressive Communication

Scholars and thought leaders have created various theories and paradigms of the different ways in which people communicate with others. There are several types of communication styles that we could identify and it would be remissive to write this section and not discuss at least one set of styles. Toastmasters International (2021) outlines four categories of communicators:

- Direct communicators may show decisiveness, competitiveness, and independence in their communications. This communicator only wants the details needed to understand the context and get the job done. Focused

on results, this person is ambitious, goal-oriented, and driven. This can sometimes come across as strong-willed or demanding, and the communicator may show signs of boredom leading to impatience when relying on others.
- Initiating communicators may show sociability, enthusiasm, and energy. Individuals with this style are often talkative, and may be seen as more focused on speaking than listening. Their fast-paced nature can come across as impulsive because they thrive on the social energy around them, and are able to share stories where they can engage socially and work collaboratively with others. They are perceived as self-assured and innovative and focused on relationship-building. Praise and approval are significant motivators for them.
- Supportive communicators reflect calmness, approachability, and sincerity. Change can be a challenge with the supportive communicator and is approached with care, thus they may appear indecisive. They prefer a low or no tension environment and put a high priority on close relationships.
- Analytical communicators are characterized by precision and logic. These communicators can be perceived as perfectionists due to their systematic nature and task-oriented focus. They are self-reliant and diplomatic, needing to feel sure of their stance and others' expectations, and do not easily express emotions or opinions.

Many of us may recognize ourselves in more than one category depending on the scenario. Clarity in communication and knowing more about who we are as communicators reduces stress for both the expressor and receiver. Knowing our personal, or individuals', communication style is one level of understanding. But recognizing the complex systems involved in wider groups of people allows us further understanding. We must account for the people in our community and understand that cultural background and communication processes will also play a role in the interpretation of messaging. In *The Culture Map: Breaking through the Invisible Boundaries of Global Business*, (2014), author Erin Meyer outlines how communication can be mapped across cultures from high-context communication to low-context communication. For those of us coming from a low-context culture, we prefer to communicate simply, clearly, and repeat the message. We do not assume that anyone possesses the knowledge we have, and so we break it down and keep things clear. However, those of us coming from a high-context culture assume that everyone shares a similar level of understanding and communication and can therefore be nuanced, layered, and sometimes inferred.

Beyond doubt, communication is far more than "one talks and another listens." There are so many influencing factors on how we wish to be communicated with and how we want to make ourselves known. When we work in environments that are people-centered like our schools, there are many factors to consider in order to understand how people need to express themselves.

▶ KNOW YOUR AUDIENCE

Think of a time recently when you read an email that left you confused or asking more questions when you were seeking answers. What about the last conversation you had with a colleague?

After the communication, how did you feel? Was your messaging clear? Did you think about the message AND the receiver of the message?

In *Simply Said: Communicating Better at Work and Beyond* (2016), Jay Sullivan emphasizes the importance of audience-centered communication. He states that effective communication involves focusing more on the audience's needs, perspectives, and expectations than on the communicator's own ideas or delivery. With that in mind, what kind of communicator do you need to be in that moment for your particular audience? Sullivan points out that many people approach communication with a focus on what they want to express rather than what the audience needs to hear. This can lead to miscommunication or messages that do not resonate as intended. Because of this, Sullivan advises to:

- Know your audience by understanding their background, interests, and concerns.

- Tailor your message by adapting your language, tone, and content to what will be most relevant and useful.
- Anticipate questions which means that you need to think ahead about what your audience may not understand and address those issues proactively.
- Engage with empathy by considering how your message will be received emotionally, and aim to connect on that level.

By keeping the audience at the center, you not only improve clarity but also foster stronger relationships and collaboration. This approach builds trust, reduces misunderstandings, and makes communication more effective overall.

In addition to this focus on the audience, Chris Fenning, author of *The First Minute: How to Start Conversations That Get Results* (2020), gives a simple framework to support clear and straightforward communication to focus on your audience.

Framing = Context + Intent + Key Message

Fenning states that it is important to frame a conversation so the purpose of the communication is clear. To frame a conversation or interaction, providing context, intention, and the key message matters. We are sure that all of our readers have experienced a meeting, conversation, or email in which one or more of these elements were missing. We know that everyone's time is precious in a school context. We want to get everyone on board, engaged, and moving in the same direction together. Having a simple framework such as this can help us be clear and intentional in our communication. Here are some examples.

Examples of communication framing when your audience is teachers:

- We are starting a professional book study with the book, *School Leadership Edit*, to learn how to be more strategic about some of our school systems. If you are interested in joining, please respond with "I AM IN" by Friday COB.
- Our staff meeting will be on Thursday at 3:30 pm in the multi-purpose room. We will use this time to go over expectations for the new science curriculum. Please bring your laptop.

- Mr. Santos has been hired as our new school nurse. Stop by to say hello, and give him the forms that parents are returning by Friday COB.
- Fred's parents dropped by to see me yesterday and were filled with praise about the work you are doing! Keep up the great work!

Examples of communication framing when your audience is parents:

- "[Child's name] has been exhibiting some behavior that may be affecting their learning and wanted to share our approach to address it. Additionally, by creating "x" structure together, we can help [child's name] refocus and stay engaged."
- "We're introducing a new reading program that focuses on improving comprehension. Please read the newsletter about how this program will benefit your child, meet school goals, and what you can do to support it at home."
- "[Child's name] has shown some recent progress in math. They have shown growth with 'x' and 'y.' By working together, we can ensure they continue to build confidence and improve their skills."

Your goal is clear communication; a clear, strong message that can be easily understood using short, simple language, focusing on the needs of the audience. Consider what you want the audience to do with your content keeping in mind that communication can just be about building rapport.

Schools send surveys home at certain times of the year for specific purposes. Our friend and author of *Chief Empathy Officer*, Thomas Hoerr, shared (personal communication, 2025) that he sent many surveys home for families at different points in the year. His purpose was to gather as much information as he could so he knew what he needed to do more or less of in his role. Offering a space to learn about what was making him effective in his role based on the feedback from parents shaped his relationship with families in a positive way.

▶ WHY DECLUTTERING COMMUNICATION MATTERS

We Need Clarity

Have you heard this phrase from author and research professor, Brene Brown: "Clear is kind. Unclear is unkind" (2018)? Clarity in communication can calm our emotional and mental state because it reduces confusion. Communication is a key factor for a positive school climate (Mousena & Raptis, 2020). If communication is fundamental in developing, creating, and maintaining positive climates, then imagine what it is like when those communication streams are clear, coherent, concise, and well-timed. Meghan Everette, Ed.D. created a framework in her dissertation research, *Mistrust and Messaging: An Analysis for Mass Communication in Schools* (2022) to support actions of well-executed and effective communication in schools. Below are the six steps for success needed for clear and effective communication:

- Audience: Think about judgments and assumptions you might make about who you are communicating with.
  - Am I assuming my audience has all the background information needed to understand this message?
  - Am I assuming all readers of this message are English speakers?
- Content: Reduce language demands, keep it simple.
  - Do I have unnecessary jargon or words with multiple meanings?
  - Did I include biased language?
- Medium: Ensure your message matches the medium.
  - Would I put the same information in a text as I would in an email?
  - How do I share the same message effectively in different formats to reach more of the audience?
- Design: Ensure readability.
  - Did I use the most accessible fonts and colors?
  - Are the images accessible?
- Time: Sending messages with consistency.
  - Did I send this message at an appropriate time?
  - Do I send messages within a timely manner?

- Plan: Develop a consistency plan.
  - Who are the members of my communication team?
  - What are our messaging responsibilities?

With these six steps, it is possible to think through and create your models for messaging to your school community members.

Lindsay Prendergast, Ed.D., Assistant Director of The Danielson Group and former principal, shares this quote attributed to George Bernard Shaw, Irish playwright: "The first problem with communication is that you think it happened" (n.d.). When Lindsay first read those words, she laughed. She "winced at the many memories they elicited of occasions when [her] communication - or the lack thereof - caused confusion, frustration, missed opportunities, and an array of other disconcerting experiences for [her] and the schools [she] led. The most important lesson [she] learned from this message, however, helped [her] on countless other occasions to be the kind of communicator who helps others feel confident, prepared, and capable of success" (personal communication, 2024).

We Need to Manage Time Waste

One solid tip we suggest to edit cluttered communication? Stop talking. Often, when we think about communication we are focused on transmitting exactly what it is we want to say. But perhaps we need to instead focus our attention on speaking as little as we can. We all know those people whose talking can make those precious minutes tick by! Hattie and Smith (2021) tell us that school leaders need to engage in more dialogue than monologue. They state that communication from leadership often has an overemphasis on monologue and a single person or group expressing directives. But instead, engaging in dialogue is a more helpful approach. Development of a listening culture is a determining factor in developing a positive school climate (Mousena & Raptis, 2020).

Similarly, instructional coach and author Jim Knight (2022) provides two main takeaways when discussing effective communication: questioning and listening. Neither of which has a focus on the speaker and instead has a focus on the audience. He reminds us, "…we need to build relationships and trust - and to do that, we need to ask great questions and listen effectively" (p. 51). Effective communication requires us to move our attention away from what we deem important to say and instead, listen, question, and engage in dialogue to build the connection we desire. Or, as Zeno of Citium said in Ancient Greece, "We have two ears and one mouth."

We can monitor our time spent talking by using the strategies above to remind us to keep our communications pared down, clear, and managed in a timely fashion.

We Need to Manage the Cognitive Load

While we may equate effective school leadership with curriculum know-how, or progress on school improvement plans, it is actually the leaders' ability to communicate effectively that is valued by teachers (Brown, 2020). When asked, teachers identify communication skills as of utmost importance for the administration. Through these communication skills, school leaders can build rapport, articulate the vision of the school, and motivate the team. Ultimately, teachers find this element of the work to be the most pertinent aspect of supporting their work in the classroom.

Knight (2021) assures us that we can learn to improve our communication skills. If we treat our communication skills like a habit or hobby we enjoy, we can develop and improve it. "We can learn to be better communicators in the same way we learn to play a sport or cook a dish" (p. 81). If we can see that being a more effective communicator can help us to improve rapport within the team, the climate of the school, and the outcomes for all community members, it seems like a worthy investment. Getting good at communicating can reduce that mental stress, if we keep practicing positive and clear communication habits.

One method that appears to be employed quite frequently in schools is the once-a-week newsletter or housekeeping notice. Superville (2022) reminds us that this can be an essentially helpful way for teachers to know when and where to find pertinent, summarized information. Receiving too many notifications will not only clutter our inbox but will also increase the chance that busy educators will miss items, or begin to tune it out. But having one reliable routine such as a weekly bulletin, will enable people to build a habit of in-taking and referring to information.

Superville also encourages school administrators to get to know the onsite staff and the way in which they may best receive information. Perhaps it is an email for the group you are working with, but it may also be a bulletin board in the staffroom, or face-to-face meetings. Communication methods may need to be modified depending on who you are communicating with and what the agenda is for the communication. In Tammy's role as Director of Teaching and Learning, she asked teachers for their preferred methods of communication: personal emails, group email, text, as well as the frequency. Knowing how teachers best needed to receive information assisted the process of communicating messages with timeliness, effectiveness, and efficiency. While this method of communicating through multiple channels seems like more work, it is not. It is possible to share the same message through different channels if you set up templates for your message, and you can schedule them in batches when you do your administrative work. This will help reduce the amount of mental effort needed when communicating with clarity.

Conversely, when what seems like an endless amount of messages are received every day, we also need to ensure that the receiver of information can intake messages easily and without interpretation. Remember, clear is kind. When people have to read or hear messages and spend their time and energy interpreting the information, this can lead to confusion and frustration. So, if you have something to say, say it. Do not leave room for interpretation.

For example, Mr. Sonos, a fourth-grade teacher, was observed and his administrator was looking for levels of student engagement. To reduce cognitive load for Mr. Sonos, the principal could say: "Mr. Sonos, many students were engaged in your lesson today. I saw this, this, and this, that led to engagement. Moments I witnessed less engagement were this, this, and this." Instead of: "Mr. Sonos, your lesson was really fun. I did notice some students were a bit wriggly and not as tuned in as others. Have you tried x, y, z....?" (long winded, rambling list of suggestions to follow). The receiver of this communication needs precise information to reduce the need to interpret and free up mental space to comprehend what the requests are from the messaging. With the direct statement at the end of specific observational notes about student engagement, Mr. Sonos can build understanding and evidence on how he knows when students are authentically engaged.

We Need to Manage "Digital Pollution"

It can be easy to forget that there are humans on the other side of our digital communications. Business experts, Ethan Beute and Stephen Pacinelli (2021), classify digital pollution into three tiers: innocent, consequential, and intentional. In schools, generally we would see innocent digital pollution in the sense that often messages received by the recipient are poorly timed and feel unwanted, despite this not being the intent of the sender. Beute and Pacinelli state that we "have not yet adapted to virtual environments ... We generally lack cultural norms, established patterns, and shared expectations to close the gaps. Most of us proceed into these spaces and behave just as we would in the real world without considering their nuances" (p. 24). As much as we try to cover all bases when we communicate digitally, is it more meaningful and accurate when we communicate in-person?

While digital communication certainly can be more convenient in terms of time use and frequency, should we rethink the use of how much we send messages through digital media? Are we hiding from having hard conversations when we send an email? Authors of *The Friction Project: How Smart Leaders Make the Right Things Easier and the Wrong Things Harder* (2024), Sutton and Rao explore how friction in communication can hinder efficiency and how leaders can become "friction fixers." They highlight key concepts to consider in organizational communication, and here we consider the two most apt for our school contexts:

- Executive Magnification: The actions of leaders are amplified due to their position. For instance, sending an email late at night may seem insignificant to the leader, but can set unintended expectations for the team. This can make the team feel obligated to respond outside of working hours. In schools, this concept applies to administrators and principals, whose behaviors can influence the entire staff culture. A seemingly small action can ripple through the school, setting informal expectations about workload, communication, and availability.
- Educational Jargon: Clarity in messaging is essential. In schools, teachers, administrators, and parents often come from varied backgrounds and may not all share the same

understanding of educational language and use of terms. Leaders must be conscious of the language they use to ensure that all constituents share a common understanding of language used in the community. Miscommunication due to jargon can create confusion and reduce trust, so using clear, inclusive language is essential for effective school leadership.

This relates back to the section earlier in the book about trust. Decluttering and editing communication is a way to build and maintain trust with your community members. These concepts remind educational leaders to be mindful of their communication habits. By understanding the impact of their actions and simplifying their language, leaders can reduce friction, foster better communication, and build a more supportive and collaborative school culture.

Through all of our analysis of research, experiences, and stories, and synthesis through conversation and ideation, we have some strategies and processes for you to think through as you streamline and clarify your communication messaging and systems in your schools.

THE 5R's: EDITING STRATEGIES FOR COMMUNICATION

Does your audience not receive your messages well anymore? Are folks not responding as you request them to? Are you recognizing that this may be a time to change your messaging, style, tone, or some other aspect of your communications? This is a good thing. You can see there is a need for change. Seeing that your messages are no longer achieving the intended goal will allow you to reimagine how and what you are communicating. It allows you to realize what barriers you may need to remove or how you can repurpose your current systems. Knowing a change is needed can allow you to recognize where to reinvest your time and what to refine.

▶ REIMAGINE

Purpose of Communication

Communication is often perceived to be for disseminating information. But consider the alternative of it being multi-directional sharing of knowledge, ideas, and concerns. Effective communication is a tool in which we can build relationships and innovate in our work. If we have worked on being clear in giving directions only, we are missing opportunities to build something better. Reimagine your communication by creating messages that directly ask for a call to action, to invite a reciprocal conversation, and get the information you need in response quickly. Calls to action in your messaging should:

- Be stated directly in the subject line.
- Be stated at the end of your message before your closing with the required details to make an effective response.
- Have a singular focus, i.e., there is only one call to action in your message such as "Please respond by [this date]," Please answer the following questions by [this date]," "Please fill in this form by [this date]," etc.

Dr. Michele Ogden, former principal of an elementary school in Irvine, California learned many lessons about communicating with her school community. She said that when communicating "with staff, I tried to keep communication to what was urgent, important, or requested by them. If I could make it an email, I did" (personal communications, 2024). When Michele planned her communication for staff meetings, she "sent them out in advance and included the type of action we would take. I noted if we were discussing, sharing information, and if follow-up or feedback was needed." She tended to communicate information when it was important, and she communicated it more than once. Even with a streamlined and focused communication stream, she reflected that "even those with the best intentions miss something in an email or forget something at a staff meeting."

▶ REMOVE

Barriers to Communication

Frances Frei (2023) stated, "[j]ust because you've said it, doesn't mean they heard it." Assuming our communication is clear whether checking if it is in fact so, is going to cause frustration for everyone involved. Our communication needs to be timely, clear, pitched carefully, and simple enough for everyone to understand.

What are some barriers we often create when communicating?

- Judgements we make about our audience.
- Assumptions we make that once you have informed everyone of something, that it has been fully heard, understood, and actioned.
- Unclear messages.
- Fonts or colors are not accessible (i.e., yellow lettering on a white background or size 10 font).
- Messages in one language.

What are some ways to remove barriers and ensure that we are not making these assumptions?

- Spend time to fully understand our audience.
- Always have someone else read your message to ensure clarity before sending.
- Use a digital resources such as Grammarly or an AI tool to check for effective language usage.
- Use the Americans with Disabilities Act Standards for Accessible Design in your message creation.
- Where possible, ensure your messages are translated for languages represented in your community.

Considering what barriers may exist and ways to remove them will ease frustration and increase clarity.

▶ REPURPOSE

Current Communication Systems

What systems are already working well in your school? And what evidence do you have to make sure that it is in fact effective? It is not enough to follow a hunch, and assume that the systems are functional. When you identify an effective system that you already have, how could you leverage this to support areas that are lacking?

Some examples:

- If the staff at your school are already in the habit of reading a morning bulletin, what information could be disseminated there to lessen the time taken in staff meetings?

- Does your staff pass through the office each day? What can you communicate on a whiteboard that does not need to be another email that you would need to send?
- Is your staff on WhatsApp? Can you send a group message with quick daily reminders?

Lindsay Prendergast, Ed.D., also shared that she categorized information, meaning, when receiving new information, she organized it by the current priority (personal communication, 2024). When sharing information, she aimed to help people with this filtering system by giving simple titles or headers in the school-wide communications such as newsletters, staff meeting agendas, and emails. Depending on the project and content, headers might be "For Awareness Only," "Action (or Response) Required," "Ongoing Topic," or "Coming Up Next." As communication cycles recurred, she used the previously organized content to move things into new categories (from "for awareness" to "response required," for example) in the next share-out as an approach to a running record that keeps topics and ideas from disappearing off people's radar.

▶ REINVEST

Tools

Reinvest in some of the communication tools that you know about and use. Many of the tools we use have more capabilities than we know exist. You invested some time in learning them initially and often we just use them as we always do. Maybe you set up your "away" message in your email settings, change your font size and a signature. But did you know that you can:

- Schedule an email to be sent at a time that suits you?
- Offer meeting times right in your email and your digital calendar for the times you are available?
- Add browser extensions like Loom to your email to create a five-minute screencast (instead of having a meeting!)?
- Add CloudHQ to your email, then record and embed a video into your email with your message?

A principal in New Jersey shared with us that they now send 5-minute video clips in an email to share information to staff instead of sharing that information at an in-person meeting. Staff appreciate that they can watch it on their own time in the suggested time frame and can refer back to it.

Tammy uses a digital tool called Textblaze that helps with time management in communications. This is an extension that allows you to create templates in organized folders. With a simple keystroke and key word combination in your messaging platform, your message will automatically populate as a draft. Having a template and making simple revisions will decrease the amount of time you use to construct messages.

Habits

Check on the last time you evaluated your communication habits. When do you write your texts and emails? When do you have in-person conversations with people? It can feel isolating to be a school leader and if you are only communicating digitally, without the human connection, you can feel further isolated. Do you have the habit of checking your email all the time? Is that helping or hindering your attention to your present communications? Think about how reinvesting in your communication habits can help you become a more focused, in-tune, and strategic communicator. Here we have an example of how you could set up your day to build in your habits:

- Morning (7:30 am–11:00 am): Email, text, make video responses to emails.
- Mid-day (11:00 am–3:30 pm): In-person conversations.
- Late afternoon (3:30 pm–5:00 pm): Phone calls, emails.

Sometimes emails are sent at times when they have the potential to be missed, or can leave people anxious about the message when received. We would suggest breaking the habit of sending emails at the end of the week or term if the content is significant or requires cognitive effort. Christine had the experience of sending out a celebration email too late in the week to be picked up on by her staff. When the message was finally read, the initial excitement had gone and the team-building moment was missed out on. Avoid this mistake by building habits around when the best time is to communicate with your team. Build the habit of sending your messages according to your edited communications plan to avoid emotional responses from staff or having your message go unnoticed.

Sharing Gratitude

At certain times of the year, it can feel easier or more stressful to communicate with your community. An email memo in September has the potential to have a very different reaction than one received in April! Is there a way to sprinkle in messages of gratitude (not just at the usual holiday times) between all of the serious memos that come out?

There are certain times of the school year that feel like a greater investment in people is needed than others. For example, once the year gets rolling past those first few team-building days, how often do you feel, as the school leader, that you do not have the same time to invest in communicating with your staff? By no fault of your own, but by nature of the role, your attention is occupied by parents, discipline, and leadership meetings, rather than focusing on expressing your gratitude to your staff.

Reinvesting in yourself as the school leader can get you refocusing on communicating with your community. Here is what you can do:

- Set aside time to revisit your communication schedule.
- Diagram or chart out what messages you share, with whom, and when.
- Make a plan for when and how to communicate.

▶ REFINE

What You Have Already Been Doing

Peter DeWitt (2022) reminds us that communication incorporates all areas of W.O.V.E.N.: Written, Oral, Visual, Electronic, and Non-verbal. How can you refine your current communication skills so that you are considering all aspects of these areas? One strategy you could employ is to do an audit of your communication skills currently, to see what kind of refining may be helpful or necessary (*New Leaders Blog*, 2024). In the space of a day or week, take note of the communication you have been involved in and which areas of W.O.V.E.N. they represent. What patterns and trends do you notice? For example, if you notice that the most consistent miscommunication is arising from your electronic messages, you can take action to improve your skills in this area. Or, if you hear feedback that you do not seem to be listening attentively in meetings, it is time to reflect on your non-verbal communication.

Time Use

We talked about the importance of managing time waste. This has been one of the most common areas that teachers and administrators have voiced that they need to prioritize in our workshops. With so many demands, and what feels like so little time, how can we refine when and how we communicate to our communities? Are you finding that you have many questions following your emails, requiring you to make more responses?

Think about:

- When am I communicating with staff?
- When am I communicating with parents?
- What time of day are my community members most likely to read their messages?
- Do I have messages batched?
- Am I having to follow up with people more often than I should?
- How can I refine my communication timelines to ensure I am communicating in a timely manner, AND communicating with clarity to reduce confusion, questions, and responses required?

LINGERING QUESTIONS

- In what ways can I evaluate my communication systems?
- When and why do I most often have to clarify my messages?
- How do I overcome barriers to communication?
- How can I get feedback on the effectiveness of my communication?

In the next chapter, we will discuss and work through the 5R's regarding school-wide expectations. As you read, spend time thinking about how an environment such as your school can simplify expectations with the goal of clarity for your community as an essential component of its success.

References

Beute, E., & Pacinelli, S. (2021). *Human-centered communication: A business case against digital pollution.* Fast Company Press.

Brown, B. (2018). *Dare to lead: Brave work. Tough conversations. Whole hearts.* Random House.

Brown, M. N. (2020). Communication for success in elementary Title 1 leadership. *Journal of the World Federation of Associations of Teacher Education, 3*(2a), 33–41. https://www.worldfate.org/docpdf/journal_03_2a.pdf

DeWitt, P. M. (2022). *Collective leader efficacy.* Corwin Press.

Everette, M. (2022). *Mistrust and messaging: An analysis for mass communication in schools* [Doctoral dissertation]. University of Florida.

Fenning, C. (2020). *The first minute: How to start conversations that get results.* Alignment Group Ltd.

Frei, F. (2023). Think fast, talk smart (M. Abrahams, Interviewer). Stanford GSB. https://www.gsb.stanford.edu/insights/simplify-how-communicate-complex-ideas-simply-effectively

Hattie, J., & Smith, R. (Eds.). (2021). *10 mindframes for learners: Teaching for success.* Routledge.

Inclusive & effective communication: 4 strategies for education leaders. (2024). *New Leaders Blog.* https://www.newleaders.org/blog/inclusive-effective-communication-4-strategies-for-education-leaders

Knight, J. (2021). The conversation workout. *Educational Leadership, 79*(3), 80–81.

Knight, J. (2022). *The definitive guide to instructional coaching: Seven factors for success.* ASCD.

Meyer, E. (2014). *The culture map: Breaking through the invisible boundaries of global business.* PublicAffairs.

Mousena, E., & Raptis, N. (2020). Beyond teaching: School climate and communication in the educational context. *IntechOpen.* https://www.researchgate.net/publication/344462739_Beyond_Teaching_School_Climate_and_Communication_in_the_Educational_Context

Sullivan, J. (2016). *Simply said: Communicating better at work and beyond.* Wiley.

Superville, D. R. (2022). Ensure your staff gets the message: 3 tips for school leaders. *Education Week.*

Sutton, R. I., & Rao, H. (2024). *The friction project: How smart leaders make the right things easier and the wrong things harder.* St. Martin's Press.

TES. (2024). *School wellbeing report 2024: International.* https://www.tes.com/for-schools/content/tes-wellbeing-report

Toastmasters International. (2021). *Understanding your communication style.* https://www.toastmasters.org.nz/wp-content/uploads/2021/12/8206-Understanding-Your-Communication-Style.pdf

Chapter 3
Editing Expectations

Setting clear expectations is essential for effective school leadership, but it does not have to be overwhelming. In this chapter, we invite you to reimagine how expectations can support both educator wellness and sustainable habits. We can start by eliminating excess, considering what and how to cut back by 50% to focus on what truly matters. Think about how to edit and transform your expectations of the Professional Learning Communities (PLCs) into spaces for meaningful collaboration, and recommit to your core values through a reflective audit, ensuring alignment with your school's mission. Making common language visible, clarifying policies and procedures following them with consistency can help move your community forward. By streamlining expectations, you can better co-create a supportive environment where both staff and students can thrive (Table 3.1).

Table 3.1 Summary of 5R's in Decluttering and Editing Expectations

5R's	Editing Strategies
Reimagine	Goals and habit principles Authentic educator wellness
Remove	Subtract 50%
Repurpose	Professional Learning Communities (PLCs)
Reinvest	Values audit
Refine	Language use Policies and procedures

DOI: 10.4324/9781003566724-4

▶ WHAT IS EXPECTED OF OUR SCHOOLS

When we consider expectations in the context of schools, various perspectives and inferences might surface. We could be discussing the expectations of students with regard to their behavior, their achievement, or their participation. We could be discussing the teacher's expectations about their professional efficacy, their development, and how they conduct themselves. We could be discussing the expectations of parents, and in turn, the school's expectations of them. Schools, as organizations, have expectations set by boards or districts, and also need to consider the expectations of their community. Expectations attached to financial responsibility, assessment achievement, and providing adequate care and support for each child are also prevalent in every school across the world.

A 2024 TES study of over 2,000 international educators found that 91% of respondents identified themselves as skilled workers and 85% felt confident in their assigned roles. These figures showed that teachers feel that they are ready and able to do their jobs well. However, only 60% reported feeling empowered in their jobs to make decisions, and worryingly, only 51% perceive their workload to be manageable. What is it then, that is going wrong when a group of people feel confident and trained in their work, yet are not feeling empowered to be autonomous, and unable to manage the workload assigned to them? What does this say about the expectations?

In addition to the wide-ranging expectations that can be present in schools, it is also important to consider the impact of expectations not meeting reality. This gap occurs when individuals or groups have certain ideas of what will, or should, happen. These expectations are often linked to their values and prior experiences. Subsequently, what actually happens in reality does not match up with what was envisioned. When there is a gap such as this between expectations and our reality, negative feelings such as discontentment, anxiousness, dissatisfaction, and depression can arise (Scott, 2022). Accordingly, the careful setting out of, communication of, and management of expectations in schools is of significant concern.

Just as the complexity of schools can make communication challenging, so can it make expectations confusing and unclear. If expectations are unclear, misunderstood, unmet, or misinterpreted, we can do just as much damage to relationships, culture, and trust, as we can with miscommunication.

Edgar Schein (as cited in Geraghty, 2023) outlined three levels of expectations embedded in organizational culture that help us to frame and understand what is present in schools. These three levels are as follows:

- Artifacts:
  - We see the explicit expectations of schools set out in documents such as policies, code of conduct, employment contracts, school logos, etcetera.
- Espoused values:
  - We are looking at the mission and vision, the values of the school, goals, school plans, etcetera.
- Underlying assumptions:
  - At this third level of organizational culture, we find the unspoken rules and expectations; the ingrained beliefs of those associated with the organization. These form over time through shared history, interactions, and observations.

Being aware of these three layers of expectations within our educational organizations can assist us to more fully understand and take action to clarify our school-wide expectations. When reflecting on this at your own organization, consider whether the expectations are aligned at all three levels and where disparities may lie. Recognizing the impact that the third layer has on all school community members, and in fact, the upper two layers, is also an important understanding to hold.

▶ TEACHER IDENTITIES

Decluttering and editing important aspects of school culture such as expectations assists in developing positive identities for educators (Suarez & McGrath, 2022). Otherwise, the weight of these over cluttered expectations can lead to predictable paths. We can support them on a path of enhanced wellness and a chance for balance, or we can keep letting educators move down the path of exhaustion.

Suarez and McGrath tell us that a positive identity as a teacher will impact student outcomes, their quality of teaching, and their longevity in the profession. They tell us that key features such as self-efficacy and belief in their own agency will contribute significantly to this. It is in the interests of all staff involved to work toward policies and practices that support positive teacher identity. And yet, how many of us could honestly attest to this being their own lived experience of the expectations placed on them?

Values

Managing Today's Schools (2022) author, Glanz, emphasizes the interconnectedness between leadership and management in modern educational settings, which can be closely aligned with establishing school-wide expectations. A framework for school leaders to create clear, supportive environments where core values such as care, community, collaboration, curiosity, respect, and compassion are consistently upheld can support clarity in speaking to and living school-wide expectations which fosters a positive and thriving educational environment.

If we revisit Schien's three levels of expectations in regards to organizational values, here is what we are considering:

- Artifacts:
  - Vision statement documents and aligned actions.
- Espoused values:
  - Confirm whether other policy or guideline documents align with your values and actions.
- Underlying assumptions:
  - What are the values we think we are living by? Here we must consider if all members of the community know the values of the school, and understand what they look like, sound like, and feel like. We cannot assume that everyone understands this. Similarly, other unwritten held values may be present, but unspoken.

When someone walks into your school, how would they know what is valued in the community? What do the walls say? What actions are exhibited by staff and students? Generally, in the schools we have worked in, the ideals and principles that matter to the members of a school community are centered on providing learners with quality learning experiences that allow for individual level of success. In a broad sense, the values of a school community are often about care, community, and learning. When your values are clear, it is possible to delineate exactly what your expectations will be (Table 3.2).

Table 3.2 Value and Expectations Alignment with Examples

Value	Expectations
Care	In our school, care means showing empathy, concern, and consideration for the well-being of students, staff, and school community members. It is about creating a safe and nurturing environment where everyone feels valued. Examples: 1. A teacher regularly checks in with students to ensure they are emotionally and academically supported. 2. A student demonstrates care by helping a peer who is struggling with classwork.
Community	In our school, our community focuses on building a sense of belonging where all members (students, teachers, staff, and parents) feel connected and involved. Everyone takes responsibility for contributing to the collective well-being of the school. Examples: 1. A school hosts regular family nights or community events where parents, students, and staff engage in activities that strengthen school ties. 2. The school ecosystem breathes inclusivity by having clubs for all types of learners.
Collaboration	Collaboration involves working together toward common goals, valuing diverse perspectives, and leveraging each person's strengths to achieve goals. Examples: 1. Teachers work in Professional Learning Communities (PLCs) to co-plan lessons, share strategies, and address challenges. 2. In the classroom, students are assigned group projects where they learn to work together by understanding group roles. They share responsibilities and contribute ideas to solve a problem.

(Continued)

Table 3.2 Value and Expectations Alignment with Examples *(Continued)*

Value	Expectations
Curiosity	Curiosity is about fostering a love for learning and encouraging students and staff to ask questions, explore new ideas, and seek knowledge beyond the basics. Examples: 1. Teachers design inquiry-based learning activities where students are encouraged to investigate topics of interest. 2. The school library supports curiosity by providing a wide range of books and resources for students to explore independently.
Respect	Respect is treating others with dignity and acknowledging different viewpoints with reciprocity to create an ecosystem where all members feel valued and heard. Examples: 1. Students practice respect by listening attentively during discussions, following classroom rules, and using kind language when speaking to peers and teachers. 2. School policies promote respect by encouraging positive interactions as a way to mitigate undesirable behaviors.
Compassion	Compassion means recognizing the needs of others and taking proactive steps to support and help them. It is the willingness to respond to suffering with kindness and understanding. Examples: 1. A school-wide initiative supports a local charity, where students and staff participate in fundraising efforts or volunteer work. 2. In class, a student shows compassion by comforting a peer who is upset or offering help to someone who is struggling with a task.

By fostering values, schools can create a positive, inclusive ecosystem that enhances both academic achievement and emotional well-being. Clear expectations AND the follow-through in actions create communities that reduce frustration, confusion, and burnout (Prendergast & French, 2022).

Michelle Jasinska, principal at Tokyo International School, shared that their learning environment and practices are:

> guided by our mission and values of providing a holistic, inclusive environment where our truly international students, staff, and families feel supported and inspired. Our expectations revolve around three core areas: creating an inclusive learning environment, maintaining consistent communication, and embodying our school's values (Trust, Inspire, Support). For students, this translates into respect for learning spaces and a focus on integrity, resilience, and collaboration. For staff, expectations are aligned with our [International Baccalaureate] (IB) Curriculum, IB standards and practice, [Universal Design for Learning] (UDL) principles, consistency in instruction, and active engagement in our community. We also encourage parents to participate in creating a positive learning environment through open, respectful communication and involvement in school events. We have a strong Tokyo International School Family Community to support this.
>
> (personal communication, 2024)

▶ PROFESSIONAL DEVELOPMENT (PD)

Hours Versus Value of Content

The Organization for Economic Cooperation and Development (OECD, n.d.) tells us that the training of teachers is increasingly viewed as a lifelong process. Continuous, quality PD plays a vital role in maintaining and enhancing the quality of education. Initial education programs lay the foundation for educators in their roles, but ongoing learning opportunities help address gaps in initial preparation, supporting educators as they adapt to evolving job demands. A lifelong learning approach to teacher development ensures that teachers can continuously refresh their knowledge and practices, fostering a dynamic and adaptive workforce. Professional development opportunities vary widely, including formal training like courses, workshops, and webinars. In more recent years, informal learning through collaboration in professional networks, reflection, podcasts, book clubs, and shared experiences has gained recognition as valuable places for professional growth.

Teachers across regions of the world have to "clock hours" of professional development to maintain certifications. In New York State, teachers must participate in 175 hours of PD over a five-year period (New York State United Teachers (NYSUT, n.d.). Teachers in Australia must take part in ongoing PD related to the Australian Professional Standards for Teachers (the Standards), an allotted time of 100 hours in each maintenance period (New South Wales Government, n.d.). Administrators and teachers in the International Baccalaureate programs must attend and receive certifications in their appropriate levels at the Primary Years Programme, Middle Years Programme, Careers Programme, and the Diploma Programme, as well as specialty certifications depending on educator roles (International Baccalaureate Organization [IBO], n.d.).

Let's play "Would You Rather?".

- Would you rather spend "x" amount of hours or "x" amount of time on professional development? OR
- Would you rather take interactive certification courses specific to your interests or your goals that fit with your schedule?

Here's another.

- Would you rather choose the type and content of the professional learning in which you engage? OR
- Would you rather be told what you have to do to reach your quota for learning hours?

Our point here is that we need to be thoughtful about the kinds of learning educators engage in. School leaders more and more are customizing professional learning for their teachers. Jill Cross, Director of Curriculum and Instruction in Memphis, Tennessee, offers targeted coaching for teachers. Jill shared that:

> [t]argeted teaching coaching opportunities are identified from anecdotal observations, summative evaluations, and professional goals. We frame professional goals using the "How might we" format, aligning with our design thinking program that follows a similar structure. Teachers collaborate with the Director of Curriculum & Instruction to determine action steps for these professional goals. In some cases, targeted individual coaching is the most effective approach, given the scope of a teacher's goals and our capacity as a small independent school. We find that a fresh set of eyes from an outside instructional coach helps to target professional growth and, ultimately, positively impacts our entire school community. This external perspective is invaluable, especially in an independent school setting where we do not have access to the extensive professional support larger school districts provide.
>
> (personal communication, 2024)

More to come on supporting staff development in the next chapter.

Hours of the "Good Stuff" Before We See Change

To achieve mastery of expectations, people need time to learn and practice the skills. Mastery depends on individual differences, the complexity of the skill, and the quality of the skill practice (Van Edwards, 2024). Each of these factors breaks down into even more specific factors for why mastery can take different amounts of time for different people. Think about this in the context of someone starting their career as a teacher. Some teachers can master specific skills very quickly. Natalie seemed to have a natural ability to establish culture, routines, and expectations with a comfortable level of ease in the first few years of her teaching career. Counter to this, Avery seemed to struggle to understand how much culture setting impacts the learning environment, and so that became a consistent challenge for her in the long term. Avery's strengths were in documentation and feedback, which she could assist Natalie in developing. In her leadership role, Laurie has been able to master the art of large-scale communication due to her background in communications with the school community within a semester. Other school leaders in her cohort turn to her for support because they find this an area in which they require a lot of support and need to focus on. The key here is to remember that teaching and leading are a highly complex science and art, and so expectations should be realistic for who individuals are. This does not mean that we lower expectations or make them too high to achieve, but we remember that there has to be a lot of the "good stuff" (quality professional learning opportunities + implementation + reflection and feedback) to see long-term change.

Support to Clarify Goals

A structure to determine how educators will reach goals provides clarity in the process of professional development and learning. Setting goals, working toward them, and ensuring that goals are aligned and maintained can be supported in-house or by outside counsel.

Tammy supports schools in a coaching role. Prior to coaching teachers, she sometimes will receive information from administrators about the specific teachers and focus areas she will be coaching. Other times she learns that she will work with teachers in a particular school and that the entire staff is working together toward the school's overall vision, values, and goals. Tammy's responsibility then is to determine the coaching priorities, focus, and goals of the individual teachers and frame it within the school's goals. Coaching conversations and sessions are fairly predictable. It is important for Tammy to know the strengths and passions of teachers before learning about what the areas for focus and growth are. There is a discussion about student work and behavior, and from there move into instructional and/or professional goals. Sessions wrap up with clear next steps: what the implementation or reflection should be in the interim between meetings, and what will be reviewed and discussed at the next meeting. Creating this expectation for the work together supports the development of a trusting relationship and allows teachers to work toward their goals strategically and thoughtfully.

▶ BUDGETS

Marrying Budgets and Expectations

Budgets drive school function. Tackling budgets can be obscure and can cause stress. Building leaders manage funds, knowing that they sometimes will not receive enough funding to meet the needs of their diverse learners (Arizona Education Association, n.d.). The systems around budgeting are highly dependent on the type of school you are associated with and where your funding comes from. If your school is funded by parent fees, or state or federally funded, or a for-profit school or not-for-profit school, will all dramatically change the way expenditures are prioritized and managed. Oversimplifying this area by proposing one strategic approach would probably be naive. But there are some universal truths to consider, no matter which school you are associated with. Things that may not be our first thought when considering budgets, but may well have a significant impact on our expectations when it comes to finances.

Financial Costs of High Teacher Turnover

One expectation that may be held in reference to school budgets is that one teacher can be replaced with another teacher for the same amount of money. Perhaps you could actually save some money if they are replaced with a teacher with less experience or certification! However, turnover in school holds a lot of additional costs, both hidden and obvious. Accepting an environment in which there is high teacher turnover is really accepting a high financial cost for a school organization.

Research completed in Alaska found that every teacher who leaves costs the district roughly $20,500. This cost covers the expenses of separation, recruitment, hiring, and training (DeFeo & Tran, 2017). The total cost to the state for teachers leaving is approximately $20 million per year.

In an international school in Hong Kong, each new teacher accrues a fee of approximately £11,500 (Steed, 2021). The principal there also highlights additional costs, such as the time taken by administration in the hiring process, the impact on the school's reputation with parents and other teachers when regarding high turnover rates, and the time taken to build an effective and collaborative team.

One district in the far north of Queensland, Australia found that in their non-locally hired teachers, 75% left within three years. In order to overcome this significant figure, they have implemented an early years careers, decade-long program focused on both the recruitment process and retention of teachers beyond three years through strategies such as tailored inductions, relationship/network building, mentoring programs, and career planning (Earp, 2023). All of which does not occur without its own financial cost.

Watlington et al. (2010) found that teacher turnover is substantial across districts and that investment in teacher retention could greatly reduce the costs associated with attrition. "Investing in teachers produces positive and exponential returns – the cost of teachers turnover is reduced and the benefits to students and society is increased" (p. 23). The authors here recommend that leaders look closely at the cost-effectiveness of teacher induction programs, as these costs may balance or minimize the costs of teacher turnover.

Strategic Approach to School Budgets

We could expect school budgets to have parallels with household budgets. We have a predetermined amount of money to spend within a defined set of time. It is prudent to allocate the money to necessities first and then use the remaining funds to discretionary items based on what seems like the most needed or wanted. Monitoring and tracking budgets is useful, especially in cases of variable income or expenditures.

Elovitz (2022) describes a common practice in determining budgeting in schools. This is where schools take the budget from the previous years and make incremental or formula-based changes based on influences such as inflation and enrollments. While this may be a time-saving strategy, it takes away the process of reflecting and evaluating how successful the previous year's budget has been and removes the voice of all other constituents in the school community.

Instead, Elovitz suggests alternative approaches to budgeting in order to focus on how a school spends its financial resources in line with its goals and strategic planning (p. 116). One strategy is described as Programming, Planning, Budgeting, and Evaluation Systems, or PPBES. This is a system in which you evaluate how well the previous budget met the needs of the community and then modify accordingly. Kagan (2022) offers another strategy called Zero-Based Budgeting (ZBB). This is a strategy to financially plan for your site, starting from a "zero base" at the beginning of each new budgeting period. This means that every expenditure for the site is analyzed for its alignment with current objectives, values, and costs, promoting efficiency in resource allocation. This approach supports streamlining documentation to expenses, with the intent of eliminating unnecessary spending.

For budget alignment, think about:

- How did we decide that money needed to be spent in a way that perhaps does not meet the needs of learners in an appropriate way?
- How can we reallocate our available resources, time use, and people to match our budget and student needs?
- Who can we bring into this decision-making process that may offer additional insight into aligning our budget with our needs?
- When did we last evaluate all of our physical resources?
- When did we lose sight of its purpose?
- When did we forget our priorities?
- When did this "maximum-ist," "bigger or more is better" society emerge in our community?
- How and why did we get so lost?

These reflection questions may have us also asking ourselves, "when, why, and how did school become so complicated?" While these approaches may take additional time, refocusing the approach back towards our purpose and priorities may end up aligning our time, effort, and finances to a streamlined approach. Here we can examine the artifacts, espousing values, and assumptions that may get us pared down.

- Budget artifacts:
  - Priorities are clearly represented in budget documents.
  - Budgets are pared down, clear, and concise.
  - Budgets are checked and reflected on during each cycle.

- Values related to budgeting:
  - Our school values align with our money expenditures.
  - Our highest priorities align with our expenditures.
- Assumptions we have when managing budgets or about how they are allocated and used:
  - We never have enough money for what we need.
  - We can not meet the needs of our population without more money.

Reflecting on these ideas may shift the way we think about budgets and how far we can stretch them.

School Accreditations

Schools seek out accreditation for a variety of reasons (Oldham, 2018). These reasons include, but are not limited to, the following:

- Meet legal requirements.
- Determining quality against a set of standards.
- School improvement.
- Earning seals of approval from outside bodies.
- Ensure graduating students have equal access to higher education.
- Marketing tool for parents.
- Accountability to districts and states.

School accreditation can take the form of self-studies, visiting teams, peer reviews, assessment against standards, internal and external assessments, or data gathering. They can be voluntary or mandatory.

The way in which school accreditations are approached and handled can solidify our expectations around our school community. They can contribute to all three levels of organizational culture, in both positive and negative ways.

An over-focus on what the accreditors want to see, or in the creation of the right "evidence," rather than the needs of students, can add pressure, workload demands, and demoralization to teachers (National Education Union, 2024). Attention, time, and effort pulled from what can feel like the real needs and concerns of the job may not be welcomed by members of the community.

On the other hand, when expectations around school accreditation are framed around self-reflection, goal setting, shared analysis to inform planning, based on actual realities of the context, we can have a very different experience of an accreditation cycle. Let us frame what the artifacts, values, and assumptions about accreditation look like so we can be clear on the expectations.

- Artifacts for school accreditations:
  - Documentation of planning, teaching, learning, and assessment.
  - Evidence of policies and practices.
  - Interviews held with different members of the community.
  - Observations of school facilities, classes, and resources.
- Espoused values around accreditation:
  - How we communicate with our community about the purpose and value of the accreditation.
  - What we do with the report/evaluation documents after they have been received.
  - Who is chosen, or who volunteers, to be a part of the accreditation process.
- Underlying assumptions about accreditations:
  - Parts of the accreditation process felt authentically valued by our community.
  - The true purpose of accreditation within our context.

Accreditation processes serve multiple purposes in the life of a school and add value to the organization when worked through with clear expectations. Communication through the process with all school community members can create a stronger sense of place and pride in the community.

▶ SCHOOLS' STRATEGIC PLANS

School leadership teams create strategic plans for schools as a way to map their goals and journey for the academic year, right? We hope so, and yet the reality might be that schools write plans with good intentions and for compliance sake. Is it possible to create clearer plans with focused expectations so the process is one that teams want to engage in for the good of the school, rather than see the process as another thing that has to be done?

Principal Jasinska uses their school values statements, strategic plans, and other school-wide documentation processes to support having clear expectations. Michelle told us that:

> [O]ur values statements and strategic plans serve as the guiding principles. In refining our documentation, I embedded language from our strategic plan and values (Trust, Inspire, Support mentioned above) to clarify each expectation's purpose, connecting it back to our mission. All strategic planning and resources are visible in shared drives that all staff can access, which helps to create transparency and keep everyone aligned. For instance, in areas like curriculum, we aligned our planning process with our definition of learning to provide clear, meaningful focus in connecting our planning with who we believe we are as learners. Whenever I recognize a need for clarification, I return to our core purpose - our mission and values - and let them guide the response.
> (personal communications, 2024)

The members of your leadership team matter. Generally, we want to include all voices from the school community to contribute to the plan drafting, yet we offer a word of caution when creating your leadership team for the purpose of writing these plans. Strategically choosing members of your team is important, as is the size of your team. How many times have you heard there are too many cooks in the kitchen? When writing school plans and expectations, you need input from your community, yet you do not need all those that provide input to be on the team. Your team will be folks who can summarize ideas and concisely write the expectation statements and documents.

Creating Plans

When creating the school's strategic plan, ask yourself three simple questions (Yoon et al., 2023):

1. "Where are we now?
2. Where do we want to go?
3. What is a credible path to get there?"

Omitting the first question can have you moving down a path that does not align with your school's value system and budget. This can cause future program and vision misalignment and perhaps community resentment. Thoughtful consideration of the third question is also vital to the process. By outlining a credible path with actionable steps, you will increase the likelihood that you will be successful in reaching the end goal of the plan. While it may be exciting to dream big, without a plausible path, we will always fall short.

Communicating and Implementing Plans

Communicating strategic plans is important to the school community and it does not have to be a complicated process. Sharing key points from the already streamlined document should allow for an easy understanding of the plan, goals, timeline, and those responsible for actionable steps. A short and focused summary email should be enough to communicate the plan.

Anyone who reads it should be able to clearly see the direction the school and its community members are taking to make incremental improvements collectively. Implementing action steps according to a timeline should be clear within the document itself. Building in more explicit accountability targets as a way to create focus can support the implementation process. This is not to create a level of distrust in the implementation, but instead commitment to school improvement and growth.

Reviewing Plans

Earlier in the book, we mentioned author Robyn Jackson and her valuable insights into developing strategic plans, particularly through her 90-day cycles of planning in "Buildership Model" (2021). How often do you meet to review your strategic plan? Do you hold regular "meeting rhythms" to maintain focus on strategic goals? Jackson explains that consistent, short meetings can help school leaders address challenges as they arise and prevent plans from collecting dust on a shelf. This approach fosters a more dynamic, responsive process of school improvement that adapts to the changing needs of the entire school community. In a time when we suggest strategically reducing meetings, these are meetings you want to keep in your schedule.

By applying these strategies, schools can move from simply setting goals to consistently making measurable progress and building a culture that supports long-term success. This is our vision for schools. Strategic plans are an expectation, and they do not have to be complicated. A short cycle review can support Jackson's model, encouraging leaders to ask the right questions, focus on eliminating barriers, and make small, continuous improvements, which ultimately lead to more sustainable school development.

Because school strategic plans and accreditation cycles drive the lives of schools, sharing a summary of the 5R's for these two processes alone seemed warranted.

The 5R's of School Improvement Plans:

- Reimagine: cycle review lengths, who is involved in the process, clarification of the process, budget spending, the school's vision, and whether our approach is proactive or reactive.
- Remove: low value initiatives, excessive budget spending, and reactiveness.
- Repurpose: documents, policies, and evidence for different audiences.
- Reinvest: in strengths over deficits, being proactive.
- Refine: clarified priorities, reflection protocols, streamlined processes, and systems.

The 5R's of accreditation processes:

- Reimagine: who is involved in the process, data collection, the school's future after accreditation.
- Remove: extraneous and unneeded documentation.
- Repurpose: documents, policies, and evidence for different audiences.
- Reinvest: in goal-setting, documentation processes.
- Refine: clarifying priorities, clarifying school community resource options.

THE 5R's: EDITING STRATEGIES FOR SCHOOL-WIDE EXPECTATIONS

As we move into some explicit identification of strategies for using the 5R's in your school, we should focus our attention on why and how clarifying, living, and revising school-wide expectations create and support the culture development of the school.

▶ REIMAGINE

Goals and Habit Principles

Oftentimes, in our personal lives, we set out goals proactively and aspirationally. We do the same in schools when writing school goals and plans. But realistically, how many times do we see these plans go forgotten, or postponed due to other concerns that arise? Often, our grand plans fall flat and we are left feeling disappointed in the failure of our plans. Because of this, it is worth considering the reasons why we can fall short of our goals. Eades (2022) outlines the top four reasons why team goals fail:

1. Clarity about the goals
2. Commitment to the goals
3. Agreement to the goals
4. Coaching to achieve the goals

We can see from this list that simply having a goal is not going to be enough to ensure success. Setting goals must be developed as a collective effort. Hearing from all constituents can ensure the success of working toward and attaining goals. The goals must be communicated, mutually agreed upon, and systematically coached to, in order to make them happen. With this viewpoint, it is clear to see why school goals and plans may not end up being achieved. We have to recognize that shared goals are something that needs engagement from all parties involved over the course of the goal timeline.

Goal setting means that we will be taking small steps to achieve a specific outcome. Whereas habit setting means that we will create a consistent routine that helps us to work toward the goal while simultaneously encouraging ongoing improvement. When we achieve a goal, we do not stop. We want continuous improvement and growth.

What are the habits you have created when working on school-wide expectations? Do you do what you've always done? Reimagining your habits can help you ensure you meet your goals. *Atomic Habits* (2018), written by author James Clear, provides valuable insights on habit formation that can be applied to creating and maintaining schoolwide expectations in a way that fosters consistency, engagement, and long-term success (Table 3.3).

Because these principles are simple, thoughtful, and require the community to be engaged, words and actions of consistency are supported. Expectations and their habit creation do not have to be complicated or convoluted.

Table 3.3 Habits for Schoolwide Expectation Development and Maintenance

Habit Principle	Examples
Make it Obvious	All staff will prioritize the use of the same online and software platforms. You have the tech department set a landing page so that when teachers log on to their laptops, it takes them to the sites and pages they need.
Make It Easy	Recurring meetings are scheduled at the same time and the same place, and can easily be shared with staff in the same way. Invitations and reminders are created automatically.
Identity-based Habits	Our professional development and learning requests require alignment with our school's mission, vision, and values.
Environmental Design	We will modify the school environment to naturally support the desired actions and behaviors. Meeting spaces will then be arranged with discussion and collaboration in mind.

Authentic Educator Wellness

Understanding that educators are people with families and lives outside school is an important part of establishing the expectations about what authentic educator wellness should look like. Anyone working in schools must be supported in the expectation that it is physically and mentally beneficial for them to detach from school responsibilities over breaks, on weekends, in the evenings, and when they need to take a health release day. Consider the artifacts, espoused values, and underlying assumptions that are held in your context around educator wellness. If the reality of your school is that there are not any artifacts that directly address educator wellness, you would not be alone. In fact, underlying assumptions about hard work and long hours are ingrained in us from our teacher training, all the way through our career. As leaders in education, what role could we play in creating artifacts to reinforce healthy expectations and potentially shift the underlying assumptions over time? In Chapter 7, we provide more insight and discussion into these supports for developing well-being.

▶ REMOVE

Subtract Expectations

Be bold and reduce the school-wide expectations by 50%, as Leidy Klotz (2021) suggests in his book *Subtract: The Untapped Science of Less*. The concept of subtracting can be valuable when reviewing school-wide expectations. Klotz argues that people tend to lean towards adding more when trying to solve problems: adding tasks, rules, and initiatives. Often we overlook simplifying, and an effective option of subtracting. In schools, this principle can help leaders streamline processes, reduce redundancies, and focus on what truly matters for student success.

For example, instead of continually adding new behavioral expectations, curriculum standards, or initiatives, schools can evaluate which existing policies or activities might be unnecessary or counterproductive. By removing certain rules or streamlining procedures, schools can reduce the workload on both staff and students, improve focus, and make the system more manageable. Subtracting reduces cognitive load and fosters a balance in the environment which supports long-term success.

Ask yourself and your leadership team:

- Which expectations are best supporting our young learners?
- Which expectations support our professional culture?
- Which of our expectations are outdated?
- Which expectations can we subtract or remove?
- How much time should we give ourselves to test if the removal of expectations is beneficial?
- How will we know if removing expectations is beneficial for our community?
- Do our existing expectations have artifacts that prove their existence?

Review these questions at your strategic planning meetings. Check in for:

- Reduced mental stress and fatigue.
- Increased focus.
- Improved school climate.
- Increased student success.

▶ REPURPOSE

Professional Learning Communities (PLCs)

How do you leverage the vision and goals of your professional learning communities? Do they align with the school's goals? Ultimately, any goal that a PLC creates should align to your school goals. How can you create a clear throughline and streamline expectations? Timothy D. Kanold, author of *The Five Disciplines of PLC Leaders* (2011), explores how school leaders can manage expectations through the Professional Learning Community (PLC) framework. He emphasizes shared leadership and collective responsibility for student achievement.

Kanold explains that establishing goal hierarchies can directly support alignment with schoolwide goals. This means that at least one goal set by each PLC should align directly with a schoolwide goal, creating "reciprocal accountability" (p. 172) and a clear expectation of goals to be achieved collectively. Using simple and consistent templates and systems for goal setting and tracking will create clarity in the team's expectation for documentation. This creates visible throughlines and can support focus on the work toward the goal. Additionally, to streamline time use and win points with our teams, review the goal progress during PLC times, rather than adding another meeting.

▶ REINVEST

Values Audit

Set aside some time at one of your faculty meetings to audit your values statements. Set up a protocol to allow staff to unpack your school values or values statements and align them with practices and implementations. What trends in thinking do you hear? Do your values still align with what the activity in the school looks like, sounds like, and feels like? If yes, celebrate your focus and share that with your larger community. If not, this might be the time to either reinvest in your statement to reflect current practices or reinvest in your practices so they match your original vision. That determination should be a collective decision. Do this work in one meeting or two consecutive meetings so that expectations are once again clear.

▶ REFINE

Language Use

It can be challenging to establish clear expectations when the school community uses different vocabulary. Establishing a common language for what expectations look like and sound like will allow for consistency in not only the heard vocabulary but also the actions and behavior of all individuals in the school community. Let us borrow three of the habit principles here for this (Table 3.4).

Policies and Procedures

Written policies, codes of conduct, or value statements; the artifacts of the organizational culture should be scheduled in for

Table 3.4 Habit Principles in Creating Expectations for Common Language

Habit Principle	Examples
Make it Obvious	Create clear and visible reminders of expectations in all common areas. Post photos of students of behavior expectations in hallways, classrooms, and restrooms with the specific wording for how to move in the halls. (e.g., Our hands stay to ourselves).
Make It Easy	Reduce barriers to following expectations by ensuring clarity and simplicity. Use consistent language across staff (e.g., "Be Ready, Be Respectful, Be Responsible").
Identity-based Habits	Shift from "rules" to creating a collective identity around schoolwide expectations. Use language like "At our school, we show kindness."

review with your leadership team. Review any items in an "as-needed" cycle based on conversations and activity, and schedule out the less-needed review items out over time. Clarification of expectations in these documents can support the reinstatement of what we want and any changes to be pursued. What refinement can you make in your artifacts?

- Are your school policies clear? (delineate major policies)
- What are your codes of conduct? (staff and students)
- What are your school values and how are these communicated?
- Do all community members have a say in the revisions we make?

Reflecting on these questions in a systematic and timely manner will support us in decluttering expectations in our documentation. Editing the load in our policies and documents will support a more streamlined and strategic approach to this big picture thinking.

> **LINGERING QUESTIONS**
>
> - In what ways can we create a stronger connection between our school's values and expectations?
> - What questions do we now have about the impact of the artifacts, espoused values, and underlying assumptions in our school community?
> - What evidence can our school produce to confirm the artifacts and espoused values around expectations at our school?

In the next chapter, we look into different avenues of teacher support such as observations, evaluations, and feedback cycles. Reading through ideas about how we can unfold more thoughtful and comprehensive support systems for teachers will get you thinking about how you can collectively sharpen what exists in your school.

References

Arizona Education Association. (n.d.). *Education funding and budget*. https://www.arizonaea.org/resource-library/education-funding-and-budget

Clear, J. (2018). *Atomic habits: An easy & proven way to build good habits & break bad ones*. Avery.

DeFeo, D. J., & Tran, M. (2017). *Cost of teacher turnover in Alaska*. Center for Alaska Education Policy Research, University of Alaska Anchorage. https://doi.org/10.15367/caepr.2017.0104

Eades, J. (2022, January 6). 3 proven leadership strategies to set your team up for success this year. *Learn Loft*. https://learnloft.com/2022/01/06/3-proven-leadership-strategies-to-set-your-team-up-for-success-this-year/

Earp, J. (2023, July 12). School leadership: Attracting and retaining teachers. *Teacher Magazine*. https://www.teachermagazine.com/au_en/articles/school-leadership-attracting-and-retaining-teachers

Elovitz, L. H. (2022). Fiscal management: Guidelines for school leaders. In J. Glanz (Ed.), *Managing today's schools: New skills for school leaders in the 21st century* (pp. 113–130). Rowman & Littlefield.

Geraghty, T. (2023, February 3). *Edgar Schein's three layers of organisational culture*. Psych Safety. https://psychsafety.com/psychological-safety-edgar-scheins-three-layers-of-organisational-culture/

Glanz, J. (Ed.). (2022). *Managing today's schools: New skills for school leaders in the 21st century*. Rowman & Littlefield.

International Baccalaureate Organization (IBO). (n.d.). *Meeting PD requirements*. Retrieved October 10, 2024, from https://www.ibo.org/professional-development/about-our-workshops/workshop-categories/meeting-pd-requirements/

Jackson, R. R. (2021). *Stop leading, start building: Turn your school into a success story with the people and resources you already have*. ASCD.

Kagan, J. (2022, March 31). Zero-based budgeting (ZBB). *Investopedia*. https://www.investopedia.com/terms/z/zbb.asp

Kanold, T. D. (2011). *The five disciplines of PLC leaders*. Solution Tree Press.

Klotz, L. (2021). *Subtract: The untapped science of less*. Flatiron Books.

National Education Union (NEU). (2024). *Majority of teachers considered leaving over Ofsted.* https://neu.org.uk/press-releases/majority-teachers-considered-leaving-over-ofsted

New South Wales Government. (n.d.). *Professional development requirements.* NSW Government. Retrieved October 4, 2024, from https://www.nsw.gov.au/education-and-training/nesa/teacher-accreditation/maintain-accreditation/professional-development-requirements

New York State United Teachers (NYSUT). (n.d.). *What you need to know: Certification & state requirements.* Retrieved October 10, 2024, from https://www.nysut.org/resources/special-resources-sites/professional-development/certification-state/what-you-need-to-know

Oldham, B. (2018). K-12 accreditation's next move: A storied guarantee looks to accountability 2.0. *Education Next, XVIII*(1), 25–29. https://www.educationnext.org/wp-content/uploads/2022/02/ednext_xviii_1_oldham.pdf

Organisation for Economic Co-operation and Development (OECD). (n.d.). *Education policy review: Reviews of national policies for education.* OECD GPS. Retrieved October 10, 2024, from https://gpseducation.oecd.org/revieweducationpolicies/#!node=41732&filter=all

Prendergast, L., & French, A. (2022, July 28). How administrators can help prevent teacher burnout. *Edutopia.* https://www.edutopia.org/article/how-administrators-can-help-prevent-teacher-burnout

Scott, E. (2022). The expectation vs. reality trap. *Verywell Mind.* https://www.verywellmind.com/expectation-vs-reality-trap-4570968

Steed, M. (2021, September 15). The hidden costs of high teacher turnover. *TES Magazine.* https://www.tes.com/magazine/leadership/hr/hidden-costs-high-teacher-turnover

Suarez, V., & McGrath, J. (2022), "Teacher professional identity: How to develop and support in times of change". *OECD education working papers* (No. 267). OECD Publishing Paris, https://doi.org/10.1787/b19f5af7-en

TES. (2024). *School wellbeing report 2024: International.* https://www.tes.com/for-schools/content/tes-wellbeing-report

Think Insights (September 4, 2024). *Schein's Organizational Culture Model.* https://thinkinginsights.net/consulting/schein-organizational-culture/

Van Edwards, V. (2024, December 10). *Here's why you don't need 10,000 hours to master something.* Science of People. https://www.scienceofpeople.com/10000-hours-rule/

Watlington, E., Shockley, R., Guglielmino, P., & Felsher, R. (2010). The high cost of leaving: An analysis of the cost of teacher turnover. *Journal of Education Finance, 36*(1), 22–37. https://www.jstor.org/stable/40704404

Yoon, E., Lockhead, K., & Kirsch, M. (2023). *The hard questions to ask about strategy. Harvard Business Review.* https://hbr.org/2023/12/the-hard-questions-to-ask-when-planning-your-strategy

Chapter 4: Editing Educator Support

Every year, you predict you will be knee deep in teacher observations and evaluations, yet it ends up being more like neck deep. This chapter invites you to reimagine the structures you have in place for providing quality educator support and think about creating systems that foster clarity and alignment. Our discussion walks through areas to eliminate stress and friction, so you can pave the way for smoother, stronger relationships, more engaging professional learning, and better instruction (Table 4.1).

Table 4.1 Summary of the 5R's to Edit Teacher Support

5R's	Editing Strategies
Reimagine	Your structures
Remove	Stress and friction
Repurpose	Multiple tools into one comprehensive one that aligns with your mission, vision, values, and population
Reinvest	In aligning time with priorities
Refine	Narrow goal setting using the "High Jump Analogy"

DOI: 10.4324/9781003566724-5

▶ THE E WORD

In the last chapter, we discussed the expectations placed on schools and teachers. Demands on schools and teachers are varied and originate from multiple circles within society. Broader society demands particular behavior, appearance, and attitudes of teachers. Our students have expectations of us, as do their families. Policy makers, districts, and boards of education create demands that certain goals, achievement targets, and the drive towards continual improvement are at the center of educator's attention. And this is not to mention the expectations that teachers place on themselves.

To ensure educators are delivering quality educational experiences and are exhibiting desired professional habits and behaviors, school leaders often lean into a particular set of metrics outlining expectations about performance to be utilized during evaluations.

Evaluations are generally a part of a teacher's year as a teaching professional. Although observation and evaluation structures and practices vary between public, private, and international schools, the goal should be the same: to improve the quality of the teaching and learning experience. With this focus, an evaluation system should clearly reflect how this can be achievable and accomplished.

▶ THE PROBLEM WITH PROFESSIONAL SUPPORT

Emotions can play a role in the mentoring, coaching, observing, and evaluation cycles. Teaching is a creative craft, science, and sport, and to many teachers, everything about their work is very personal. Decluttering the emotions around teaching performance can shed some of the burden of the support cycles. The understanding that all educators need support, some support looks the same between colleagues, and some looks different. Later in the chapter we share ideas about bringing staff into the process more and developing trust so that evaluations and support can be effective, objective, and personalized, yet with the intent not to be taken personally.

Another major issue we face with evaluations is that they can take copious amounts of time in the administrator's schedule and mental space. In the podcast episode titled "Rethinking Teacher Supervision, Coaching & Evaluation" from The RocketPD Podcast (Marshall, 2024, 00:15:30), Kim Marshall mentions that school leaders spent approximately six hours on observations and evaluations per teacher. PER TEACHER. This is a substantial amount of time spent when you have a small staff of 20 teachers, and what seems like an astronomical amount of time when you have a large staff of 100 AND have multiple administrators supporting the process. Knowing this, we need to understand how to declutter and edit this process to make this cycle of school improvement more time-efficient and still effective.

▶ WHAT IS "SUPPORT"?

We want to bring to your attention the use of the word: support. Generally, a support is any tool or action that helps someone. To have a strong and robust support system, and truly empower the teachers within it, we need to define the structures that drive the whole process and system. Without a clear direction and understanding, support processes may not be equitable or meaningful. Let us define what we mean.

Mentoring occurs when a teacher is matched with another teacher who has more experience than the other. The mentor serves as a model and "expert" for the teacher who has the lesser experience or needs greater support.

A coach provides targeted and focused support for their coachee. The coach asks the coachee several types of coaching questions such as directive, facilitative, or reflective, depending on the needs of the teacher. Although there are different types of coaching, essentially the goal is that the coachee will eventually answer and come to the realization about the shifts they need to make in practice. This is facilitated through the questions and reflection protocols used by the coach through an inquiry stance for providing support.

Observations are visits to classrooms that evaluators and administrators make to gather observable data about instructional practices and student engagement and behaviors. Observations may also occur when colleagues visit other classrooms to learn from other teachers.

Evaluations are the process for providing feedback to teachers about the observations and are used as a formal part of the process for determining a teacher's goals and tracking their professional growth.

Personalized professional development and learning serve as the foundation for educators to become effective practitioners by learning about leading, teaching, and learning in ways that are the most relevant for them (Table 4.2).

Table 4.2 Types of Teacher Support

Type	Benefit	Challenge	How to Edit Support
Mentoring	Provides less experienced teacher a partnership with a more experienced peer	Added responsibility for mentor, time	Create a schedule with clear expectations
Coaching	Provides non-evaluative feedback and thought partnership	Ensuring all staff have a coach, acquiring coaching skills in limited time	Create clear expectations and focused action steps, hire an external coach
Observations	Provides formal and informal feedback from coach or supervisor	Feedback may feel personal or subjective, scheduling	Focus on only observable actions and heard words
Evaluations	Provides objective and formal level of teaching proficiency	Can cause stress, maintaining trust and a growth mindset through challenging conversations	Use a research-based or co-created tool as a source of objectivity

Because all teacher support systems require much communication, it is important that we highlight a key idea from Jim Knight, founder of Instructional Coaching Group and author of many coaching books. In his book, *Better Conversations: Coaching Ourselves and Each Other to Be More Credible, Caring, and Connected* (2016), Knight outlines how to have hard conversations. Hard conversations can absorb a lot of time and require much energy. If we are clear on the intent of the conversation, we can support those that we are having those tough conversations with. Knight favors listening as a priority in conversations with those he coaches. As school and instructional leaders, we experience all kinds of conversations with colleagues, and not all of them feel productive and positive. However, when we keep several key ideas about how to navigate difficult conversations, we can move through them with less stress and clearer focus. Here is a summary of what Knight suggests:

- Listen with empathy, be curious, and non-judgmental: Listen first and then ask open-ended questions.
- Focus on problems to solve and goals: This shifts the focus from blaming people to a focus on solutions.
- Be prepared: Having some anticipated responses written down with your key points will keep your conversation on track.
- Use your emotional intelligence: Check in on your emotional stance and center yourself before a conversation to stay focused on goals and priorities.

▶ WANTS IN SUPPORT CYCLES

It can be easy for us to identify what the problems are in our roles, no doubt, so here we will shift to what educators want and need to support professional growth.

What Teachers Want

Let us speak frankly about what teachers want when they need support. Realistically, some teachers would choose to opt out of the evaluation process because it can feel overwhelming, judgmental, and not helpful. Yet, evaluation cycles have immense value when done well (Stronge & Tucker, 2003). For teachers who welcome the process, they want useful feedback, ideas, and strategies to try in their classrooms. They want follow-up and continued support for the work they do every day. They want support that fits their needs in a timely fashion. They want a short and logical cycle that helps them make the necessary improvements in their teaching practices (personal communication, n.d.). They do not want to be judged and questioned. They do not want to waste their time with supports that are not targeted. Keeping the evaluation process simple and decluttered can keep teachers and evaluators focused on improving the teaching and learning experience.

Former school principal and author, Dr. Thomas Hoerr, shared with us a simple action his teachers appreciated in their evaluation cycles (Musiowsky-Borneman & Arnold, 2025, 00:20:12). His candid, empathetic, and informal approach to sharing and discussing feedback for observations was taken as a way to build and sustain the relationships built between teachers and himself. This approach reduced stress and formality yet still offered the same result, offering time for reflection and constructive feedback from an observed time in the classroom. He shared with us, "My job is not to make everybody happy. My job is to create a setting where everybody grows. And empathy is a key, key, part of that because I need to know who you are, what you value, and what is important to you and how I can help you."

After multiple conversations with educators, time and again, we have heard from teachers in many pockets of the teaching world about what they want from their school leadership teams (Arnold, personal communications, 2024). Teachers want:

- trust and a level of autonomy,
- time to plan and collaborate with colleagues,
- guidance and support when faced with challenges,
- high-leverage strategies to increase student engagement,
- and tools and tips that help them streamline their work and become more effective.

What School Leaders Want

After having coached or led teachers in some capacity in numerous schools and speaking with principals, they often have a common response when asked what they want from teachers. School leaders often say they want teachers to care for their students, be open to learning, and be dedicated to improving their teaching practice so that students engage in the best learning experiences possible (personal communications, 2024). Who can argue with that? We know it is idealistic to say this, and yet it is different to wish it into existence. The hard part is not getting teachers to care, because we know they do care for their students. The hard part can be the latter. It can be hard when it is time to look at practice, evaluate, reflect on, and implement change, AND maintain that, all whilst nurturing professional relationships. Principals have voiced that they want their teachers to feel encouraged and confident in their abilities and be comfortable in taking risks and responsibility in what and how they teach.

Tools for Support

The reality of teacher evaluations is often more complicated than it needs to be, causing stress for the evaluator and the teacher. Using a framework can help reduce some stress and ambiguity in this process. As a former classroom teacher in New York City, Tammy and her colleagues were introduced to the Danielson Framework in the late 2000s. This framework outlines four domains:

1. Planning and Preparation,
2. Learning Environments,
3. Principled Teaching, and
4. Learning Experiences.

These domains are to support developing teacher practice and include specific indicators for growth. The beauty of the framework is that there is a clear, progressive focus for teacher direction and progression of skills. With focused use, this is a valuable tool to support administrators and teachers in the professional learning process. Like any tool we use in education, we must proceed with caution. Without the time to learn the tool, process the language, and understand its value to one's practice, its use can be lost. Focusing on too many domains or indicators in observations, and during pre- and post-observation conversations, can muddy the waters.

A leadership team must decide and communicate how the tool will be used for observations. The Danielson Framework is intended to be used as a tool to support professional growth (Prendergast, personal communication, 2024), yet is often used as an evaluation tool which leans into "leveling" teachers and creates feelings of animosity toward a tool or framework such as this.

A recommendation we have if this is the case at your site, your leadership team can create a simple evaluation tool based on the Danielson Framework. For example, if the focus of a teacher observation is Domain 1: Planning and Preparation, and specifically 1b: Knowing and Valuing Students (Danielson Group, 2022), then your evaluation checklist will only include the descriptors under this category. Chunk the descriptor to keep the focus on the intended language, behaviors, and actions. It can become easy to start looking for too many of these elements, resulting in an unfocused observation. Teachers need and deserve focused and explicit feedback on chosen goals, whether they are school-wide goals or classroom-level goals.

An example might be:

> Domain 1: Planning and Preparation, and specifically
> 1b: Knowing and Valuing Students
> - Respect for Students' Identities.
> - Understanding of Students' Current Knowledge and Skills.
> - Knowledge of Whole Child Development.
> - Knowledge of the Learning Process and Learning Differences.
> (Danielson Group, 2022, p. 12)

Each of these four statements includes a description of what this looks like for an unsatisfactory through distinguished teacher performance. There is one statement per indicator and each is focused for that performance level. While it may be the goal to have a teacher work holistically on 1b, perhaps one of the indicators is the focus per set time frame and over time the teacher has worked on all elements.

To reduce some of the stress, school leaders can invite teachers into the conversation about what the focus will be during observations. Teacher involvement in determining domains or indicators for growth promotes the trust and care needed to effectively support teachers within their role, which is often highly personal to them. Using artificial intelligence can also be used to help with the tone in the written feedback, if that is a point of worry for you or teachers when sending and receiving feedback.

To make her observation and feedback rounds more time-effective, Jamilah Parker, Supervisor of Early Childhood in New Jersey, uses the Danielson Framework and AI tools to write concise feedback for teachers (personal communication, 2025). Once she has her collected observations, she writes the feedback she wants to give teachers, and she inputs it into AI to write succinct feedback comments for them. Teachers have shared their appreciation for the feedback when Jamilah meets with them during post-observation meetings.

Leader Evaluations

Much like teachers, and employees in any industry, leaders must have an evaluation and feedback cycle to gauge effectiveness. As a teacher, Tammy had a vision of who she needed her school administrators and instructional coaches to be. Not who Tammy wanted, but who she needed, to support her colleagues and herself with their professional growth. They needed their school leaders to:

- understand the dynamics of their classrooms,
- support their capacity as the instructional leader in their classroom,
- support their team as a teaching unit,
- create equitable opportunities and resources to become better teachers,
- provide them with timely and helpful feedback,
- and share and support the implementation of schoolwide systems that made sense for their community.

During that time, Tammy assumed her administrative team knew how to support teaching staff, and specifically what she and her colleagues needed. The layers of teacher support needed in any school are vast and varied, and she had not anticipated whether or not her school leaders were, in fact, getting the support they needed to effectively support teachers. Regardless of in-district growth opportunities and support for school leaders that are context-specific, it is important to note and be aware of tools created outside your district or region.

The Illinois Principals Association published the "School Leader Paradigm" (2022, p. 27), which serves as the framework for their new evaluation plan. It details the personal intelligences a learning leader must possess (the Becoming side) and identifies the skills within three domains (Culture, Systems, and Learning) and twenty-one dimensions (the Doing side) the leader must develop to lead an effective learning environment. This is designed as a comprehensive framework to support the development of school leaders throughout their careers, and outlines a progression through four career stages: Aspiring, Launching, Building, and Mastering, each with specific competencies and intelligences to be developed. By integrating personal, social, and systems intelligence, the principles behind this framework encourage leaders to become effective learning leaders who can transform their schools into the desired dynamic learning organizations many aspire to develop. This structured approach ensures that evaluations are not merely compliance driven but are instrumental in fostering meaningful professional growth, thereby enhancing the overall effectiveness of educational leadership. While the document is lengthy, it is worth looking into Part 5 to learn more about the six-pronged framework for leader development.

With this, think about your school site and ask yourself:

- Do I have an evaluation and support system for myself and people in school leadership positions?
- What is our process for evaluation and feedback?
- How often do I ask staff to support me with my growth?

Thinking about this perspective, can that help you shift your thinking about how you implement support cycles for your staff?

Decluttering Support

In *10 Mindframes for Leaders*, Mitra et al. (2021) emphasize the importance of building relationships and trust to create a safe learning environment where both teachers and students feel comfortable making mistakes and learning from one another. We can thank Carol Dweck for much of this work related to the growth mindset about the importance of learning from mistakes, which is prevalent in so many of today's schools. Mitra, Hattie, and Smith's approach fosters open communication and collaboration, enabling teachers to receive constructive feedback and support, which enhances their professional growth and effectiveness. We know that by cultivating trust, leaders support the personal empowerment of teachers to experiment with new teaching strategies and share what they have implemented. Over time, this will lead to improved student outcomes. Many of us have long known that prioritizing trustful relationships is essential for leaders aiming to support teachers in their professional development.

Tammy had a positive and normally productive relationship with her administrators when she taught in a large school district in a diverse urban environment. She and her co-teacher were comfortable in being observed and were often looked to as models for instructional practices and routines. However, for one observation cycle, Tammy was made to feel not only disappointed, but also as if she was not capable of doing her job well. Teachers at her school were to choose between formal or informal observations and part of that evaluation process included pre-observation meetings, observations, followed by post-observation meetings. In this instance, Tammy chose a formal observation and submitted a math lesson plan prior to the lesson to be observed. When Tammy received the lesson plan back, she expected some feedback to think about before the observation. Instead, written on the plan was the comment, "do you have enough clocks?". Disappointed with this unhelpful question, Tammy experienced doubt in her capability to be prepared for lessons when she normally would not have. This contradicted the fact that her class was often visited by outside school guests. Tammy looked forward to comments or questions that would potentially enhance her planning and the learning experience for her students. This instead made her rethink the type of observations she would choose in the future and in the subsequent years she chose the path of informal observations. This eliminated the time it took to prepare a formal lesson plan and have pre-observation meetings. She opted instead to leave less chance of confusion, and less feelings of stress because she would teach as she normally would. However, she may also have missed opportunities for rich, meaningful discussions with leadership because of this chosen pathway.

Let us come back to this idea that trusting staff empowers them to grow professionally in their roles and learn from mistakes where necessary after reading this example. Further to Mitra, Hattie, and Smith's ideas, Dr. Paul Browning (2020) has claimed that "[o]ffering trust doesn't mean that there isn't accountability or support for growth; it means allowing others to do the job they are employed to do and, if necessary, allowing them to experience failure" (para.7). So then, how does a growth mindset and trust help us declutter the support systems we have for teachers? When we trust our colleagues, our levels of stress are reduced because we know that there is accountability and follow-through. This removes layers of complicated conversations and what can feel like a lack of understanding of the teacher's ability to plan and deliver meaningful instruction. Authentically trusting someone changes your relationship with them, resulting in more focus on priorities and less attention to minutia.

Here we will revisit more ideas from authors of *The Friction Project* (2024), Sutton and Rao. The authors share how "The Help Pyramid" (Chapter 3) can make school and teacher evaluation systems more user-friendly and adaptable by addressing both the interpersonal and structural challenges within these systems. Here's how each layer of the pyramid can contribute:

1. Influencing Others, or the bottom three layers, are what we view as foundational in building trust and strong relationships.
    - Supporting: Encouraging empathy, understanding, and practicality helps school leaders and evaluators build trust with teachers, making feedback more constructive.

- Guiding: Providing clear, personalized guidance ensures teachers understand evaluation criteria, reducing ambiguity and fostering growth.
- Coaching: Offering coaching opportunities allows for two-way dialogue, empowering teachers to identify solutions collaboratively, which reduces resistance to feedback.

2. Preventing and Curing Friction, or the top two layers, are what we view as proactive and thinking ahead to avoid anticipated snags.
    - Preventing: Designing transparent, flexible, and growth-oriented evaluation processes helps mitigate misunderstandings and friction before they arise.
    - Curing: Addressing conflicts promptly and constructively helps restore relationships and system trust, ensuring evaluations remain productive and positive.

Authentic Support

In *The Minimalist Teacher* (2021, p. 63) and in the introduction chapter of this book, we mentioned Rogers' Diffusion of Innovation and the idea that on any staff, we will always have a range of how people will react to adopting new ideas, practices, or changes. Our teachers have a lot of responsibilities, and so we can think about how the range of teachers will respond to knowing and understanding that all will participate in professional learning.

- New teachers: Generally eager and open to learning and trying all they possibly can, but may not be able to see into a deeper level of integration and skill transfer yet.
- Mid-career teachers: Often open to digging deeper into research and strategies that make teaching more authentically engaging and enhance learning at a high level, but may have specific areas of interest that do not match the school's vision right now.
- Veteran teachers: Have the wisdom to connect new learning with previous professional development, but may share that they have already experienced the things you are saying and have existing processes that work for them.

How we respond to these reactions can make or break the professional learning experiences and cycles for any teacher.

Years of productive, clear, and what seemed to be effective evaluation cycles, as well as the not-so-great ones, informed the structures Tammy adopted and implemented as a Director of Teaching and Learning, when coaching new and veteran teachers. The structures and systems implemented were based on authenticity, simplicity, and a level of informality for which teachers responded positively to. Teachers signed up for meetings and observations. At meetings, teachers shared their goals, strengths, and challenges. In this role and her role as coach, during observations Tammy observes requested areas of challenge or desired growth and follows up with teachers via email using a simple "Glow, Grow and Next Step" reflection. Teachers respond to the emails with reflections and questions, and at the subsequent meeting, Tammy and the teacher discuss implementations based on the last observation. The process is simple, focused, and fluid. Although the coaching sessions and observations are not used for evaluation, they support teachers in the evaluation process they undergo with their evaluators.

Teacher support can feel flimsy and inauthentic if teachers do not have some options and agency in the process. Effective teacher support is strategic, straightforward, and can offer options for authentic opportunity for growth. Supporting, coaching, mentoring, observing, and evaluating take time and cannot be done effectively without trusting relationships. So how can school leaders build trust, save time, and still help support and develop teachers' effectiveness? Consider the following:

- Offering Master Teachers to become informal evaluators to do observation and provide feedback.
- Partnering teachers to observe each other and give feedback.
- Creating a scheduled timeframe for teachers to video one of their lessons, watch it for self-reflection, and chart out instructional shifts.
- Offering quick turnaround time for observation and feedback cycles.
- Offering an 80/20 approach for professional learning and development (more on this in the 5R's).

From ideas shared in *Managing Today's Schools* (Glanz, 2022), we can see that schools today are reconceptualizing the roles of principal and teacher, as we see and have experienced shifts in the learning environment and landscape. In other words, reversing, in a sense, the notion that the principal is the chief leader and manager of a school. Rather, shared responsibility for change and improvement is at the core of the educational process in a school. Utilizing these varied methods of observation cycles to share the work, development and learning, can be a fortuitous experience for others to take on.

We strongly support practices that are time-saving and efficient, resulting in effective systems. A randomized field trial across four school sites by Kane et al. (2020) evaluating the impact of substituting teacher-collected videos for in-person classroom observations was worth consideration. This study indicates that when teachers recorded their lessons on video and subsequently reviewed them with a feedback partner, they experienced greater satisfaction with the evaluation process and exhibited higher retention rates compared to those who did not participate in video observations (Boryga, 2023). In addition to this, researchers highlighted that video observations improve efficiency by allowing observers, such as busy school leaders, to offer focused feedback at their convenience, eliminating the need for lengthy, in-person classroom visits. However, because there were no measurable improvements in student academic achievement or classroom experiences, it is suggested that the video feedback may need to be paired with specific instructional support to enhance student outcomes.

To further build opportunities for authentic support for teaching staff, we can look to Martin Seligman's PERMA (2011) model. This framework cultivates positive well-being and happiness. Cycles of observations are most often paired with a format or template of discussion questions to guide the cycle. Utilizing Seligman's PERMA model to frame these discussions could assist in building an authentic, trusting lens in which to guide the process. PERMA means:

- Positive Emotion: Enhancing well-being by cultivating gratitude, savoring the present, and building optimism for the future increases positive emotions.

- Engagement: Immersing oneself in a challenging task by applying skills and attention leads to the gratifying state of "flow," where the activity becomes the reward.
- Relationships: Strong relationships amplify joy, provide support during challenges, and contribute to well-being through connection, kindness, and shared experiences.
- Meaning: A sense of purpose arises from being part of and serving causes larger than oneself.
- Accomplishment: Seeking mastery, achievement, and success for their own sake provides satisfaction, even if it does not result in immediate positive emotion or meaning (Penn Arts & Sciences, n.d.).

Keeping the PERMA model in mind can help us create an efficient and effective system for supporting teachers. We know it is possible to reach all of our teachers in the most authentic ways possible (Table 4.3).

This approach promotes a culture where evaluations are seen as supportive, adaptable, and integral to professional development, rather than punitive.

Table 4.3 Using a PERMA Model to Co-create Personalized Evaluation Cycles

	New Teacher	Mid-career Teacher	Veteran Teacher
Positive Emotion	Excited to be a teacher, willing to listen and try whatever comes their way	Feels like they know and understand how teaching and learning work synergistically	Feels valued and like a contributing member of the community over a long period of time and has seen many changes
Engagement	Prioritize learning curriculum and students	Co-create and lead professional learning communities	Review systems, give feedback to leadership team

(Continued)

Table 4.3 Using a PERMA Model to Co-create Personalized Evaluation Cycles *(Continued)*

	New Teacher	Mid-career Teacher	Veteran Teacher
Relationships	Build relationships with those on their team and those veterans	Focus on building and maintaining existing and new relationships for the collective good	Support new teachers in developing relationships with their teams and promote reaching out to veteran teachers to mentor
Meaning	Develop values as a teacher	Revisit values and purpose of teaching	Revisit values and purpose of teaching
Achievement	Sees progress in understanding teaching and learning as a result of dedication to personal growth and learning	Sees professional growth clearly, and student progress as a result of dedication to own learning	Sees professional growth, growth of the team, and student progress as a result of dedication to own learning

Now that we have reviewed and discussed core components of professional learning, let's capture that with the 5R's.

THE 5R's: EDITING STRATEGIES FOR YOUR EDUCATOR SUPPORT SYSTEMS

Perhaps your system for teacher support needs some editing because the structures have been the same for a long period of time, or you are carrying them over from the last school leader.

This can be well and fine in some circumstances, yet we need to remember that you are not the same leader as the previous one, and it is unlikely that all the teachers on your staff are the same as they were a few years ago. Using the previous discussion and the 5R's, you can rethink some of the areas of "stucky-ness" you might feel when supporting the range of teachers you have on your staff. Reflecting on and editing your teacher support systems may be needed to move forward with more clarity and sustainability.

▶ REIMAGINE

The Structures

What observation and evaluation structures are offered at your school? Think about how you can take a structure that requires many meetings tied to observations, and reduce the amount of time it takes to meet and the number of times you meet to give feedback. With your teachers, co-create a plan that makes the best sense for your teachers. System-wide structures are sometimes dictated in evaluation processes; however, if you have some flexibility to adapt to your teacher's needs, do so.

Here is how your current system likely looks:

- Pre-observation: Short conversation about what you are observing based on your observation tool (i.e., student engagement, transition routines, language use, or questioning techniques).
- Observations: Hour long visit with a focus on discussed observables from your designated tool.
- Post-observation: In-person meeting using protocols for discussion.
- Follow-up: Teacher implements and provides reflection and feedback via email.

Think about the "how's" within the main structure of your observation cycle. Can you universally design a menu for this process, giving staff choices in how they share with you, are observed by you and how the feedback is conducted? Allowing for choice and flexibility encourages agency and personal preferences from staff, but may also free up time from your own schedule.

- Pre-observation: teacher emails or sends a voice note about their plan ahead of time, you respond with an acknowledgement, question, or comment. This could be in a share document that you can both add to or comment in.
- Observations: teacher videos the lesson, you can appear live, or watch it together later.
- Post-observation: you send feedback via a short video in an email or in the shared document. This can open a conversation that can extend past the traditionally allotted post-observation meeting time.
- Follow-up: teacher implements feedback and communicates the results in the shared document, during an informal chat, or during a scheduled meeting of choice. Feedback can be integrated into professional goals for the upcoming year.

▶ REMOVE

Stress

Your staff is not solely relying on you to ensure that support is in place. It is a collective responsibility so you can take that weight from your shoulders. Keep. This. Simple.

Ask yourself:

- How can I support teachers in the ways that they need support?
- Who can you bring in to support me with this?
- Do I have a form for teachers to voice their support wishes to me?
- Do I know the HOW's that match their WHAT's?

Shifting the ownership can also change what you need to do in your leadership role. Have you heard of the 80/20 rule used by many organizations and companies? Italian economist Vilfredo Pareto coined the term when he learned about the ratio of land owned in Italy versus the number of owners (Borad, 2022).

The Pareto Principle has been adapted to many industries and aspects of our workplaces. In education, this principle may appear as Genius Hour for students, a time in which students work on passion projects for 20% of their academic time. In regard to teacher professional learning time, perhaps an adapted 80/20 rule is adopted. If you follow the 80/20 rule, this would mean that 80% of the professional development time would be the school's choice, and 20% would be the teacher's. Would it be possible for school leadership to shift some of the time ownership, to say, 50% of the staff development is the school's choice, and the other 50% is maintained through teacher choice? What makes sense to you for your staff, and with your existing mandates and initiatives? We not only view this as removal of stress for you but also a repurposing of your time spent.

Friction

We previously mentioned the "Help Pyramid" from the book *The Friction Project*. Friction, according to Sutton and Rao (2024), occurs when obstacles are put in front of people resulting in slowing them down. Friction can make their jobs more difficult and potentially more frustrating. We can anticipate friction that may occur in observation, feedback, and evaluation cycles, and so we can glean some insights from Sutton and Rao's work and synthesize it with our understanding of decluttering our processes. Ask yourself the simple question: What is causing the friction in this process? Answer this as simply as possible. Once you identify the friction point, determine whether you can eliminate it or whether you need to address it. For example, you may be experiencing friction as resistance from a teacher, scheduling, or limited access to resources. Consider whether these can be eliminated or need to be addressed and then you will have a clearer path to follow.

▶ REPURPOSE

Existing Tools

Do you have multiple resources to evaluate teachers? Perhaps you are a Project-Based Learning school and use their teacher performance rubric. Perhaps your lower school is Montessori-style. Maybe Marzano is an option. Think about the benefits of evaluating the existing tools you have access to and work on creating one comprehensive tool that aligns with your school's mission, vision, values, and population.

What processes can you put in place to open this option to staff to co-create a tool? Co-creating your tool and resources will focus you and your staff on what you value in your environment and for your learners. When Tammy was Director of Teaching and Learning, she co-created a teacher reflection tool for teachers using a combination of teacher rubrics. Ideas were synthesized and adapted from rubrics and continuum tools such as the Danielson Framework and project-based learning schools. Christine was also involved in the creation of a similar tool, directly built from teacher standards framed from the school's value statements. Evaluating these tools then helped teachers align their instruction and planning for effectiveness to the school's mission, vision, and values.

▶ REINVEST

In Aligning Time with Priorities

Perform a time audit to see how your time is spent in general and then how you spend your time when you are in observation, evaluation, and support cycles.

- How much time do you spend doing teacher observations, evaluations, and all that comes with this process?
- Is your time used effectively?
- How much time do you need to invest?
- Does this time use match the priorities of your role?

We mentioned bringing in Master Teachers as personnel resources and video recording devices as tools to relieve some of the time and energy you spend on your teacher support structures. By starting, implementing, tweaking, and maintaining some of these different options, you are buying time back for yourself by aligning your time with your priorities.

▶ REFINE

Teacher Goal Setting

Teacher goal-setting processes can vary widely. Sometimes the process can become unwieldy and add extra unnecessary complications. Or perhaps your experience is that your goal-setting processes are too vague and lack specific checkpoints or timelines. Thought is needed in how to narrow the criteria and focus on how we can support teacher performance development. We are reminded of the "high jump" analogy used by Eades (2022). Using said sport to spark an idea, leaders are encouraged to intentionally explore crossbars, standards, and shelters to encourage people to work at their very best. It is important for leadership to consider the crossbar that the athlete needs to clear (the goals or expectations we want to achieve), the standards that adjust the height of the bar (clear procedures and understanding of how to reach the goals), and the shelter that forms a safe place to land (the safe and trusting culture that allows people to take risks and challenge themselves). In order to achieve success in the high jump we cannot blindly throw ourselves toward the bar and hope to beat world records. Likewise, when supporting teacher development in our schools, we need to proceed with some thought and planning. As Jones et al. (2022) captured so eloquently, "[l]eaders who communicate a clear vision, demonstrate a strategic way for everyone to meet high expectations, and ultimately get results, are the ones who garner trust and deep working relationships." Keeping this analogy in mind, and the concepts of the crossbar, the standards, and shelters associated with it, can provide a streamlined concept of how we foster teacher development through goal setting in a refined way.

> High Jump 1: Crossbars
> Guiding Questions: What is the goal the teachers are working toward?
> Your Response or Action Plan:
> High Jump 2: Standards
> Guiding Questions: What are the steps, procedures needed to reach this goal? What does success look like?

Your Response or Action Plan:

High Jump 3: Shelters
Guiding Questions: How can we provide a safe place in which to work toward this goal?
Your Response or Action Plan:

> **LINGERING QUESTIONS**
>
> - What support processes are currently in place that are too bulky, complicated, or time wasting?
> - How can we reconceptualize how we do observations and evaluations?
> - How can we personalize our processes for observing and evaluating teachers?
> - How can I share this responsibility of authentically supporting teachers in their growth with my staff?

In the next chapter, we will discuss what we think is one of the greatest challenges in the role of a leader – scheduling and time use. Many of us ask for more hours in a day; however, what we really need is to be more strategic with how we use our time. Let us work through what this might look like for you currently, and pick out some strategies you can try.

References

Borad, S. B. (2022, June 21). *Pareto principle – Meaning, history, 80/20 rule and example*. eFinanceManagement. https://efinancemanagement.com/costing-terms/pareto-principle

Boryga, A. (2023, August 4). 23 ways to build and sustain classroom relationships. *Edutopia*.

Browning, P. (2020). Teachers' bookshelf: Leadership and trust. *Teacher Magazine*. https://www.teachermagazine.com/au_en/articles/teachers-bookshelf-leadership-and-trust

Danielson Group. (2022). *The framework for teaching (draft)*. https://danielsongroup.org/wp-content/uploads/2022/06/2022-Framework-for-Teaching_Draft_June-28-2022-.pdf

Eades, J. (2022, January 6). 3 proven leadership strategies to set your team up for success this year. *Learn Loft*. https://learnloft.com/2022/01/06/3-proven-leadership-strategies-to-set-your-team-up-for-success-this-year/

Glanz, J. (Ed.). (2022). *Managing today's schools: Successful strategies for school leaders*. Routledge.

Illinois Principals Association. (2022). *School leader evaluation plan (draft)*. https://ilprincipals.org/resource/1096/School_Leader_Evaluation_Plan.pdf

Jones, J. M., Vari, T. J., & Hamilton, C. (2022). *7 mindshifts for school leaders: Finding new ways to think about old problems*. Corwin.

Kane, T. J., Blazer, C., Baird, M. D., & Staiger, D. O. (2020). *Remote observations of classroom teaching (ROC-T): A randomized trial*. Center for Education Policy Research, Harvard University. https://cepr.harvard.edu/files/cepr/files/kane_et_al_remote_observation_2020.pdf

Knight, J. (2016). *Better conversations: Coaching ourselves and each other to be more credible, caring, and connected*. Corwin.

Marshall, K. (2024, June 24). Rethinking teacher supervision, coaching & evaluation. In the RocketPD podcast: Real talk with educators. *RocketPD*. https://podcasts.apple.com/gb/podcast/episode-4-rethinking-teacher-supervision-coaching-evaluation-w-kim-marshall/id1757677291?i=1000662435143

Mitra, S., Hattie, J., & Smith, R. (2021). *10 mindframes for learners: Teaching for success*. Routledge.

Musiowsky-Borneman, T., & Arnold, C. (2021). *The minimalist teacher*. ASCD.

Musiowsky-Borneman, T., & Arnold, C. Y. (2025, February). Unlocking empathy in educational leadership. In *The minimalist educator podcast*. Buzzsprout. https://www.buzzsprout.com/2189953/episodes/16469695

Penn Arts & Sciences. (n.d.). *PERMA™ theory of well-being and PERMA™ workshops*. https://ppc.sas.upenn.edu/learn-more/perma-theory-well-being-and-perma-workshops

Stronge, J. H., & Tucker, P. D. (2003). *Handbook on teacher evaluation: Assessing and improving performance*. Eye on Education.

Sutton, R. I., & Rao, H. (2024). *The friction project: How smart leaders make the right things easier and the wrong things harder* (Kindle Ed.). St. Martin's Press.

Chapter 5
Editing Your Time Structures

As we move into the 5R strategies for rethinking and decluttering your time in your role, we realize that we are discussing a construct that often feels out of our control. We cannot slow or speed up time. Time feels like it flies by and we wonder what happened to it. What we can do as much as possible is make yourself accountable for making the most efficient use of the time you have in your role and in your school building (Table 5.1).

Table 5.1 Summary of the 5R's in Editing Your Time Structures

5R's	Editing Strategies
Reimagine	Time spend
	Your timing
Remove	Unreasonable expectations
Repurpose	Calendar use
Reinvest	"Micro-moments"
	Invest, don't spend
Refine	Time blocking

▶ TIME IS A CONSTRUCT

We use time to organize, measure, and make sense of a sequence of events. We also use time to measure the intervals between events. We often describe time as a construct because it represents a conceptual framework developed from the ideas of humans. While the passage of time is real, our perception of time is shaped by social, cultural, and historical factors (Rovelli, 2018). Factors such as these have seen that school calendars are approximately 180 days and the daily school timetable usually spans from 8 am through 3 pm. These are facts. But our experience and our perception of time are that planning periods or class blocks seem to fly by. Whereas a staff meeting may feel like it drags on endlessly. Why does this happen to us?

Thanks to brilliant thinkers, we have seen many iterations of time telling devices and event tracking systems. Just think about how our time trackers and planners have changed in your lifetime alone, and also within the context of your career in education. Now, both Christine and Tammy live by their digital calendars to track events, meetings, and Zoom links. They also keep paper calendar planners to track plans and events, including other details needed to ensure that all the minutia is taken care of for any given day and upcoming event. Tammy relies on her phone and her smart watch for the time and calendar reminders. Christine could not get by without her laptop with built-in apps for scheduling, note taking, and prioritizing and tracking tasks. Comparatively, when Christine and Tammy started their careers in the late 1990s and early 2000s, they relied on their analog watches, the classroom clock, the school bells, and hand-written paper planners. Imagine that!

▶ THE PROBLEM WITH HOW WE USE OUR TIME

How we think we use our time and how we actually use it are two different things and because of this, we suggest a time and tool audit. Auditing your time allows you to see how and where your time expenditures lie. Many of us may not be conscious of our time use, and therefore it would be beneficial for any of us to reflect on and review how time is spent. Before we get into the details of a time audit, let us first dig into some of the cultural aspects of what we encounter in our roles and in our personal lives that can lead us to what we think is a better use of our time.

Cult of Busyness and Hurry Sickness

"How have you been?"
"Sooooo busy!"

You have had this conversation before, are we right? The discussion revolves around one or more people discussing how their lives are overscheduled and busy. They can barely keep up with the demands and activities taking over their lives. These people may well have fallen into what some call the "cult of busyness."

In *Cult of Busyness,* Ben Brearley (2021) describes the signs of a cult of busyness to include the appearance of, or actuality of, a busy workload, spending long hours at work, frequent discussions about being busy, and busyness equaling value or worthiness. He warns that in work environments that highly value being busy, thoughtful work suffers and stress rates rise, all without much real evidence that we are actually getting more work done. Have you asked yourself: "What did I even do today? I have been running all day and I know I did a bunch of things, but I can not remember what." This may be a cautionary signal that our minds are too busy and our days are too full to have reflective time to think about the accomplishments of the day.

Cardiologists, Friedman and Rosenman, coined the phrase "Hurry Sickness" to describe those of us who chronically feel short of time and endlessly try to cram as much as possible into everyday life (Cox, 2022). Sufferers experience time urgency, always needing to get things done without pausing or rest. The resulting effects are stress, anxiety, panic, and irritability, and the impact on us becomes not being able to relax and sleep well. Relationships suffer and physical health can eventually also be affected, with these cardiologists noting their patients have raised blood pressure and heart problems.

Now, we will never be ones suggesting that educators are not actually busy with their workloads! We know the demands are high and the to-do lists never ending. It would be a struggle not to feel some sense of time urgency in the work that we do. It is useful to be aware of this culture around busyness and the value that it holds for many in society.

Awareness can assist us in being thoughtful about our own role within this expectation. Perhaps we should be asking ourselves:

- Are we contributing to these trends, cults, and sicknesses?
- And if so, in a helpful way or an unhelpful way?
- Can we challenge ideas that equate busyness with worth and instead embrace the worthiness of rest and time to welcome other activities in our lives?
- Can we recognize the signs of hurry sickness within ourselves or those around us?
- What can we do to combat this?

Awareness will help us regulate and monitor our levels of busyness with the intention of creating space for doing less.

Productivity Trends

The idea that our rate of productivity will have enormous benefits for ourselves and the people around us is enticing. Have you ever found yourself getting pulled into this lure of the variety of productivity trends? Productivity culture tells us that we will feel better about ourselves if we get more done, and that being productive is a more valuable trait than other attributes. If we can use the right tool or system, and optimize how productive we are, we will be our most effective, result-oriented self.

Unfortunately our reality as educational leaders and teachers is that there are always limitless tasks to do in our work. There is no amount of productivity tricks or strategies that will allow any of us to reach the end of these tasks or to feel completely in control of our time and responsibilities. We need to learn how to be more comfortable with the fact that some things will just not get done. Some things will slide. We need to ensure that what does get our time and attention matches our most pressing priorities. The hope being that not all that slides off our plates are our personal priorities.

Additionally, there are some tasks that we can not apply a productivity mindset to. We can not schedule or somehow strategically time manage the building of relationships. We may not be able to attempt much of anything requiring creativity in a rigid time block. Measuring output or statistical growth will not give us the holistic picture of success in the work that we are doing. Being the first to arrive and the last to leave, while existing on little more than coffee, does not equate to doing the best possible work in a highly active, human-centered, and engaging field such as this.

While we are not arguing that you should ignore any and all productivity trends, we will argue that they need to be eyed with thoughtfulness and caution. While we outline ways we could flexibly apply some tips and strategies, we are conscious that not all workplaces, roles, and individuals will be able to utilize these in the same ways. Your time is invaluable and it needs to work for you. Explore those productivity trends and systems, but ensure you are being reflective about what works for you and what is enabling you to be strategic and successful in your work.

The number of productivity trackers and trends has increased dramatically over the course of our careers. With role changes, the need to manage tasks, to-dos, and responsibilities within our schedules has also changed. While some tasks remain the same, an increase in responsibilities has occurred due to role demands and expectations. No matter the number of tasks and responsibilities, the amount of hours in the day has remained the same. In those early career years, both Christine and Tammy were able to manage their responsibilities and schedules without many productivity tools. Now we have a large bank of what we could potentially call productivity distractions that are there to "help" us. For example, Tammy was looking for a tool to help her track tasks within larger projects. She opted to test out digital tools such as Asana and Click-up. While both tools gave her the support she would need to track and time plot, she was not sure the time investment in learning a new tool was worth it. She opted to create similar types of tracking in an editable sheet, a tool she was already familiar with and determined would likely support her tracking the way she needed. Learning a couple of new tips from testing the other platforms gave Tammy some ideas to add into her existing tools. This helped her stay pared down and stick with a tool and system she was already familiar with and suited her needs for the time being. Updates in some tools and strategic time use, however, have allowed Christine and Tammy to manage leadership and life responsibilities effectively. Both have learned from experts in and out of the field, and have been guided in their work with others. But the key element here is that thoughtful consideration of these tools and trends has been applied to make them work for us, rather than being controlled by them.

▶ THE TRUTH ABOUT A LEADER'S TIME

There is never a doubt that there will be curveballs in the schedule of a day. Whether it is your car getting a flat on the way to school, a serious student concern, or an invitation to a grade one publishing party, your time at school is never dull. What we need to remember is that a school leader is not a superhero. They do not transcend time and space, although it may seem like they do. What many school leaders do well is manage a tricky schedule and make it look like it is just in a day's work, and to an extent it is. Yet, behind that "ease" is a person who is stretched and really just wants to get the most out of their time while in school and work with a team that equally values their finite and precious time together.

Honoring Time

What reactions and emotions are elicited when faculty meetings start or end late? We can say with certainty that there are strong, negative emotions (personal communications, 2024) attached to this behavior and this affects the community's culture (Hanson, 2024). What does lateness signal? Generally, the time of the other is not valued or important. Now, we know that there are exceptions to lateness, however, in many circumstances, we can avoid being late when we are prepared and when we have boundaries. There are only so many times you can blame traffic or the "quick" conversation in the hallway. Ms. Watson wants to talk to you about her son's not-so-serious behaviors as you are about to meet your staff for a meeting. Ms. Watson will have to wait. Having a boundary and a protocol to set up meetings will curb some of this time loss and interruption. Impromptu conversations and meetings are sometimes unavoidable, depending on the circumstance. In an emergency situation, a second protocol, such as a meeting leader designee who can take over the meeting is needed to avoid lateness and interruptions. More to come on boundaries with our "No" Rubric later in the chapter.

Trustee of Others' Time

Effective use of a school leaders' own time is a big consideration. But equally worth considering is the way in which the decisions and efforts of leaders impact the time spent by those around them. One way you could view a leader's position is as a "trustee of others' time" (Sutton & Rao, 2024). The way in which you work can have the potential to save others time and make the time they have at work the most impactful and gratifying. You could also stand in the way of effective time use by wasting time, disrespecting time, or halting progress to a standstill. To a large extent, the resource of time in our schools is in the hands of our leadership.

By the very nature of the work that we do, some tasks in schools necessitate fast, effective decisions, and task completions. Other work requires time for thoughtfulness, discussion, analysis, and reflection. It is one of the great challenges of leadership to know when different approaches to time are needed, and how to honor those needs. Additionally, you balance the need to bring the diverse people around you along on the journey, without rushing some or boring others with a slow pace at the same time.

Some questions to reflect on how we guard the time of our teams could include:

- How well am I modeling effective time management for others?
- In what ways am I empowering the team to take ownership of their schedules?
- When I schedule an event that involves more than my own time, how do I ensure it is meeting our priorities productively?
- How am I fostering punctuality and accountability with time?
- Have I taken the time to thoroughly understand the legal requirements of the teams' contracts in regards to working hours, breaks, and flexibility in work?

- Have I investigated, reflected on, and listened to others in order to understand the unspoken/unwritten culture around time use at this school?

Time Crunches Change Our Roles

In his book, *The Definitive Guide to Instructional Coaching: Seven Factors for Success* (2022), author Jim Knight discusses how his work with coaches inevitably leads to a discussion around a similar challenge – time. In fact, he mentions how feeling short of time is a big reason why many coaches leave their roles. Knight suggests considering time management in two different categories. These categories are: internal and external dimensions. The external dimensions are the time demands that are possibly out of our control, that may be influenced by people or systems above us. This may include your contract hours and the schedule within that day. Or how many staff members of teams you may need to work with, or meetings that are a requirement of the position. Whereas the internal dimension is those items that are within our power to be thoughtful about and to make intentional decisions with. Such as the way in which you manage and use the time that you do have a say over. Our discussion here will focus more on the internal dimension of your time. Shifting your external dimension is context and role dependent, and is therefore challenging to tackle in these pages.

▶ SHAPING LEADERSHIP TIME

Is it possible for our school leaders to make their time at school a little more routine and mundane, in the best way possible? Here we will review some ideas for becoming more strategic about how your time is planned for and used. If you do not plan your time, someone else will hijack your time from you. This is one way to lose intentional and strategic time use.

Time Blocking

Time blocking and boxing may seem to be counter to the to-do culture which we know so many of us live by, yet author Nir Eyal (n.d.b.) argues that the real change in our productivity and time use comes when we manage our calendars and not to-dos.

If you have ever explored the world of productivity tips and strategies, you may well have come across the idea of time blocking. This is the idea that you pre-plan your day or week with blocks of time allocated to the tasks that are required for your work. You would take your to-do list or tasks in a project and block off your schedule in order to focus and complete your to-dos. Some proponents suggest also utilizing the times when you know you will be more alert to do certain concentrated tasks, and your less focused time to do less demanding tasks. With time blocking you can reduce decision fatigue by always knowing what you will be doing, battle stress, and reduce distractions and procrastination (Ross, 2025). You can also time block tasks beyond work in order to ensure that your work-life balance actually happens. If you have pre-planned that family time, exercise, or hobbies, it will more likely occur than if you just wait for when you have the time or energy to do it.

While reading about this time management strategy might be interesting and spark a curiosity to give it a go, those working in education will probably quickly pause. The notion of having that much autonomy and say in how you spend your time in a week may well seem like some fairytale dream! Whoever created the start and end times of your school day probably did not give a lot of thought to when you feel most productive, and most certainly, that student needing first aid will not care much about it either. Even if you are the one creating the school schedule, you may have little choice about when you can fit in use of facilities or working days of staff. Depending on your role, you may have little choice about how much time you have in front of students, or how much time you have to get administrative duties done. You may have meetings or committee responsibilities that are beyond your control. There may be tasks that feel like less of a priority for you, but have a deadline nonetheless.

This is where caution and thoughtfulness need to come into how you consume time management strategies and tips. If you have the kind of role where this could work for you, then dive right in and give time blocking a go. But for those of us who have less say in our work week, we need to think a bit differently. Perhaps your school could start a "no-meetings" day of the week when you can actually allow yourselves a bit more say over the tasks that you tackle. Perhaps you apply the time blocking only to the before-or after school blocks of time, knowing that your attention is likely to be pulled elsewhere during the school day. Or perhaps you utilize the idea of time blocking only for your personal time outside of school to ensure you are having a rich, gratifying life outside of the workplace. Finding what works for you and giving yourself some time to try out different approaches will be key here.

Having said all this, there is a key point we want to bring to your attention about time management techniques. Whether you use time blocking, or another technique called time boxing, using set periods of time for specific tasks to stay focused, "you must identify your values, which are attributes of the person you want to be. Values are not end goals or outcomes, like being wealthy. We never achieve our values—just as we don't say we've achieved 'determination' by finishing one goal" (Eyal, n.d.a.). Many of our role responsibilities may not be end goal-centric, but instead ongoing processes that drive the work we do. Therefore, our time blocks may be repetitive. This itself shows the value you place on routine and in giving attention to priorities such as greeting staff and students each morning, or holding meetings only on specific days of the week because it works best for the staff.

Time Audit

To do a simple audit of your time use, look at your calendar and determine if you have a running to-do list, or if your time is specifically scheduled to do particular tasks at certain times. If you are time blocking, evaluate how you use the time. Tammy evaluated her time and created three categories: time for creative tasks, for consuming information and learning, and time for collaboration. This specific time blocking strategy allowed Tammy to see how her time blocks were allocated and helped her determine how she should prioritize her time so she was not only doing one type of work or task, and avoiding others that required more time, mental energy, and attention.

Planning out a week may be a helpful practice in order to keep our schedules tightened, clean, and streamlined with the intent to examine the actual time spent at the end of each week, before planning the next week. Long-term responsibilities can be planned back from the due date.

To audit your calendar and/or time use, we suggest reviewing your role in six categories. Within these categories, jot down how much time your tasks actually take versus your scheduled time, and ask yourself a few associated questions.

- Administrative tasks – How much time is spent on paperwork, emails, or other administrative responsibilities?
- Daily activities – What are your primary tasks each day?
- Planning time – How much time do you allocate to planning your day/week?
- Interruptions – How often are your administrative/instructional periods interrupted?
- Meetings – How many meetings do you run weekly?
- Student engagement – How much time is spent on redirecting or managing student behavior?

Reflecting on our time spend can help us be more mindful of how we use this valuable resource, so we suggest pairing your time audit with the time audit reflection and action plan in Table 5.2.

We know that reflection on our practices provides us with valuable insight into the work we do, and in this case, how we spend our time.

Time Chunks versus Time Confetti

If you are unsure whether time blocking or boxing is for you because you live by your to-do list, we do have some ideas here. Because many people rely on a list to help them track tasks, let us have a look at some strategic ways to make a "to-do list" better.

A commonly held notion that we have heard from so many educational leaders and teachers, and have felt ourselves, is that there is never enough time in the school day to get everything finished. Let alone enough time to balance school work with a personal life! Yes, we may have small sections of time allocated throughout the week for our multitude of tasks, and we wcertain work done too. Realistically, how often are we paralyzed by

Table 5.2 Time Audit Reflection

Category	Questions	Reflection	Action
Administrative Tasks Time Allotted: ___ Actual Time: __	How much time is spent on paperwork, emails, or other administrative responsibilities?		
	Which of these tasks can be delegated?		
	Which of these tasks can be streamlined?		
Daily Activities Time Allotted: ___ Actual Time: __	What are your primary tasks each day?		
	How is your time with staff spent?		
	How much time is spent on non-primary tasks (e.g., transitions, tedious duties)?		
	Are there strategies to make transitions more efficient?		
Planning Time Time Allotted: ___ Actual Time: __	How much time do you allocate to planning your day/week?		
	Are there tasks that take time away from your planning efforts?		
	Could planning time be more efficiently organized?		

(Continued)

Table 5.2 Time Audit Reflection *(Continued)*

Category	Questions	Reflection	Action
Interruptions Time Allotted: ___ Actual Time: __	How often are your administration/instructional periods interrupted?		
	What are the common causes of interruptions?		
	How much time do these interruptions take up on average?		
Meetings Time Allotted: ___ Actual Time: __	How many meetings do you run weekly?		
	How many meetings do you attend weekly?		
	What is the average duration of each meeting?		
	How many meetings directly support your school's goals?		
Student Engagement Time Allotted: ___ Actual Time: __	How much time is spent on redirecting or managing student behavior?		
	Are there patterns in when or why engagement issues arise?		
	Is there a need for policy review and community reintroduction?		

the sheer number of things that need to get done, that we do not make best use of the time we have?

A simple sorting approach may help us avoid this paralyzing feeling and work more strategically. We can categorize the way we use time into two main ideas: time confetti and time chunks. Time confetti is the idea that due to the busy nature of modern lives interspersed with technology use, we often find ourselves with various very short sections of time throughout the day. These short bursts of time may be our own, but there are only some tasks that could be logically tackled within that time. Time chunks, however, are when we find ourselves having longer stretches of time that we could use to apply ourselves to more challenging or cognitive tasks.

What if you thoughtfully used this knowledge when we consider our to-do lists? We could take our messy, unruly, and lengthy to-do lists and simply categorize according to whether it is accomplishable in a time confetti break, or a time chunk break. Categorizing our to-do list in this way will remove the challenge of not knowing where to start when we have time available to us, particularly when we have an unexpected bit of free time come our way (does that happen?!). Take the following sample to-do list as an example:

Friday to-do list:

- Email parent volunteers about book week activities.
- Update report writing guidelines with dates for this academic year and share with staff.
- Observe Ms. Phillips.
- Complete observation paperwork for Ms. Phillips.
- Watch child protection webinar.
- Contact the communications team for a meeting next week.
- Respond to Supt. Smith's email about school-wide event.
- Lend a copy of *The Learning Game* to Mr. Greeson.
- Review application forms for the admissions team.

After a simple re-categorization, here we have the Friday to-do list using the concepts of time confetti and time chunking.

Confetti:

- Email room parents about book week.
- Email Supt. Smith.
- Contact communications team for meeting.
- Drop off book to Mr. Greeson.
- Review application forms for admissions.

Chunks:

- Watch child protection webinar.
- Observe Ms. Phillips.
- Complete paperwork for observation.
- Update report writing guidelines.

My overwhelm now feels reduced, and when my meeting with the Board ends five minutes early, I have a quick go-to to feel like I am being productive and getting items off my list.

Tammy evaluates her time blocks, time use, and task list often to ensure that her calendar reflects the work she completes. This has also become her tracking system. She tracks the steps needed to complete longer term projects and blocks or boxes time accordingly. As projects progress, she evaluated the tasks, time blocks, and boxes to ensure she is making the best use of her time. It is important for all of us to remember that when we progress with projects and we take steps to achieve goals, our action steps change, and so we must modify our time blocking, boxes, or confetti according to changes in tasks.

Imagine you are working toward a collective professional goal of creating and sustaining more collaborative meeting time for teachers to share and grow professional practice. Initially, it seems as though it will work within the schedule to create and dedicate a 60-minute time block every Thursday afternoon for grade-level team meetings. During the first week, the time block works as planned. Teachers collaborate on the predetermined topics from the list of choices. During the second Thursday meeting, a district mandate requires all schools to implement a new assessment system. This task is time-sensitive, and training must happen yesterday. The planned collaboration blocks must shift to accommodate this. As a flexible leader, you adjust your blocks to boxes. On Monday, 30 minutes in the morning is scheduled to meet with the leadership team and create an implementation plan for the assessment. From Tuesday-Thursday, the Thursday 60-minute collaboration block becomes 2 × 30 minute boxes, "confettied" over three days. Thirty minutes is used for reviewing student work, and the other 30 minutes for small group teacher training sessions on the assessment system spread over three days.

Buffers

In *The Minimalist Teacher* (2021), we brought up the idea of buffers in schedules when planning curriculum and instruction. Planning buffers in your schedule is essential in keeping your schedule and events on track. Kahneman and Tversky (1979) first discussed a "planning fallacy" in their research on prospect theory, explaining how people often underestimate the amount of time it takes to complete tasks because we do not take into account types of risk factors. The study by Parker et al. (2007) links the idea of people planning to a "best-case scenario" to personality traits and cognitive biases.

Now, think about how you plan your day.

- Where are buffers planned in your schedule?
- Do you have buffers planned between calls, tasks, and movement?
- How long are your buffers?
- Are your buffers a realistic amount of time to give you time to move, go to the bathroom, eat, drink water, and/or reflect?

Buffers take time in your day and offer you a realistic sense of how your time is used, and "where your day goes." Planning in buffers is a way to help you feel successful instead of always feeling like you did not get everything done in your day.

Top Three Priorities

Productivity expert, J.D. Meier (2010), encourages people to focus on a "Rule of 3" system to help you focus and simplify the work you need to get done. The "Rule of 3" is as simple as it sounds. He suggests identifying three priorities, achievements, or wins for each day. He argues that this simple strategy will help establish a vision for the day, create meaning, and feelings of accomplishment. The "Rule of 3" can help us move away from feelings of chaos into a clearer picture of where we are going.

We can personally testify for the power of this straightforward approach. Christine often jots down her three priorities onto a sticky note at the start of the day. Walking out of the building at the end of the day having crossed off those three items, really does have a significant impact on how you feel about how your day went. While there will probably always be more on the to-do list, knowing that you have accomplished those top three priorities does leave you feeling more effective and productive. You can more comfortably accept that the work day is done, when you know those three items are checked off.

You may also like to use a daily sticky note system. Or perhaps you can leave space at the top of your day planner to write three items. If a digital planner is more your style, you can color-code your top three items for the day to make them stand out. Or perhaps you can share your top three priorities verbally over breakfast, immediately adding in an accountability partner in the process!

What Does It Look Like to Be Done?

Another twist to the top three priorities list is to consider what it would like to be "done for the day." Often we come to work having a vague idea of what needs to get done on this day, or for the upcoming events on the horizon. But we may not have essential must-do items that can be tracked, measured, or targets to be met to know we have completed our job for the day. This is one of the unique elements of our work that workers in other fields may not experience. This murkiness can ultimately make it very challenging to actually know that you are done for the day. When there is always something else needing adjusting, updating, or contacting, how do we decide if our work is actually finished?

McKeown (2021) encourages us to actually take the time each morning to decide what being done looks like for the day. Envisioning what "done" is going to look like, and agreeing to it for yourself, allows you to have a vision for the day and assists you in making the decision to wrap it up and head home. Obviously you will need to proceed with some realism when you are picturing what being done will look like. If, when writing this book, we envisioned being done for the day as completing an entire new chapter, we would be setting ourselves up for failure. Being realistic about what is achievable will need to be utilized in conjunction with imagining what being done looks like in order for this to be a successful strategy.

Delegation

Are you the go-to person whenever something happens in the building? Does every question about student learning, contracts, staffing, student behavior, duty rosters, and budgets go directly to you? With a single person being the go-to on all matters, you create a bottleneck in the school. This bottleneck not only affects decision making but also output, accountability, and efficiency (Hoff, 2019). If this sounds like the case at your school, you may need to rethink the delegation of tasks in your school community. Davies (2024) suggests instituting a "first responder" system in which it is clearly communicated who is the designated person to take questions and concerns. Take some time to establish this system and ensure it is quickly available so that you can utilize others in the building and simultaneously give yourself back some time. You will have the chance to use your time to have a greater impact, but you will also develop the skills, confidence, and strengths of the staff members around you.

If you are going to make more use of delegation, ensure that you are comfortable transferring over control of that task in more than just name only. Yes, you will need to continue with communication and sharing of key information. True delegation though, requires an extension of trust and a sharing of responsibility. Trying to maintain control of tasks you have delegated will erode relationships and result in you being seen as a micro-manager instead of an empowering teammate. Trust your team to get the job done well and reap the benefits of a shared workload and distributed leadership.

A Back-Up Schedule

There are often days when your schedule does not go as planned, are we right? What can we do to avoid a complete schedule hijack? Many of us live by one master schedule. But what happens during a derailed day when multiple teachers are absent, you have district meetings, are set to meet with the PTA, or you have a late start on a snowy day? The back-up schedule is to ensure the least amount of essential learning time is lost. Authors of *It's Time for Strategic Scheduling*, Nathan Levenson and David James (2023), suggest having an alternate schedule to avoid complete upheavals in your day.

When creating an alternate schedule, consider the following:

- Creating a shared student redistribution list in the event that substitute teachers are unavailable for coverage.
- Reducing transition time or creating shorter blocks (i.e., after a short morning meeting or homeroom time, students do not move classrooms for specials or other classes) to allow for a shorter school day.
- Shifting what happens when (i.e., right after morning meeting, start instruction on the subject or content that often gets dropped).
- Delegate your staff or shuffle your staff into different "positions" for welcoming, supervisions, and dismissal to ensure all key jobs are covered in cases of absence.

Adapt a back-up schedule that fits your school context and the events that are most likely to happen for your community. Having a prepared back-up schedule will support your community in carrying out a day that feels less chaotic and more calm.

Utilize a "No" Rubric

We know that with time restraints, it would be impossible to say yes to all requests, initiatives, and meetings. Even if we wanted to, there simply is not the space to fit it all in! But knowing when to say no, and being comfortable on the decision to say no, can be a tricky point for many.

In a blog post on newleaders.org, a "no" rubric is described as a useful tool to embrace to help with this difficult process. They suggest using a short list of questions that will help you decide what you could say no to.

Building on this idea, we have created our own version of a "no" chart to help you make quick, insightful decisions to choose what can be taken off your plate. You could use this, or work from this framework to create your own (Table 5.3).

Table 5.3 "No" Chart for Quick Decision-Making

Criteria	Guiding Statement	Yes/No
Purpose	This task directly moves our school toward our purpose of improvement.	
Priorities	This task aligns with my current priorities.	
Pared down	This task is, or can be, pared down to the essentials to ensure effectiveness.	
Potential for delegation	I am the only person who could complete this task effectively.	
Urgency and importance	This task is both urgent and important to do now.	
Opportunity cost	There is nothing of greater importance that will need to be cast aside to complete this task.	
Guarding time	This task honors the best use of both my time and the time of others.	

Once consideration of each request has been filtered through this checklist, you should be able to see the best way to respond. If you have answered mostly no to these guiding statements, then you have a clear "no" answer. If you have mostly yes responses, then this is clearly an important task you need to sign onto. A mixture of responses might mean this could be rescheduled for another time, or find another staff member that could assist and work with you on this task. Whatever the outcome, you also now have a clear reason to explain the answer you are giving!

THE 5R's: EDITING YOUR TIME STRUCTURES

▶ REIMAGINE

Your Time Spend

In Table 5.2, we shared six categories and questions to begin your time audit: administrative tasks, daily activities, planning time, interruptions, meetings, and student engagement. If you have already worked through the table of suggested questions and have started the evaluation process, you are on your way to understanding "where your time goes." Note that the question list is not exhaustive, however, we wanted to ensure the questions were few and focused to get you thinking about your role in leadership and how your time is allocated and actually spent. An audit will give you the opportunity to reimagine and potentially reallocate your time. Once you have done your audit, you can work on your modified time blocking or confetti to ensure you are meeting your goals and expectations successfully.

Your Timing

Here we are focusing on tim-ING, not time itself or your use of time. Can we assume that you have some routines and habits that feel like they are no longer serving you? Perhaps it is not the routine or habit itself, but WHEN you are engaging in it. Author Daniel Pink (2018) shares plenty of ideas about when might be the best time to do something in your work role, or with your personal life in his book based on chronotypes and circadian rhythms, *When: The Scientific Secrets of Perfect Timing*. Each of us experiences a similar flow to the day: the peak (usually morning), the trough (usually midday), and the recovery (usually end of day).

These daily patterns offer us incentive to do particular tasks and make decisions at certain times of the day versus others. We should be doing the more challenging tasks, have the more meaningful conversations, and making thoughtful decisions earlier in the day during our peak time. Trivial tasks should be done during your trough, and then you can end your day with some more thoughtful or creative work as you are in your daily recovery. This will ring true for most people, however, there are some of you out there for which this pattern may be the opposite! What we would like to point out here is that perhaps as you do your time audit, you also take note of WHEN you are doing the tasks that require the deepest thought.

Assistant Principal Kennedy blocks his calendar each day from 1:45 to 2:15 pm to read and respond to emails. What he has noticed about this routine is that he finds it challenging to read with focus and create thoughtful responses to those emails, but instead, he can do a quick check to ensure there is nothing urgent. This could be because he has reached the trough in his day. He decides it might be a better plan to read and respond to his emails later in the day, after his recovery time, or when he arrives at the school before everyone else and he is at the beginning of his peak time.

▶ REMOVE

The Unreasonable Expectations

We have walked through ideas from the culture of busyness and potentially toxic productivity, which we can informally define as viewing all circumstances as positive, rather than viewing the reality of circumstances and working through them realistically. Thinking about where you fall within those thoughts and behaviors, remember to be kind to yourself. Remove the unrealistic expectation of yourself and potentially from others that all parts of your schedule are filled with completing observations, in meetings, or doing paperwork. We say this with a sense of lightness, but this really does mean – stop yourself. Tell yourself that you are placing unrealistic expectations upon yourself. Tell yourself no. In your time blocks, you need time to process through all your encounters in a day and have some time for reflection. This will make you more present and help you become a more attuned leader. We ask that you do not beat yourself up when you do not get everything done, or seemingly can not meet the unreasonable and unrealistic expectations you have set for yourself, or others have of you. Instead, reflect on the positives, the accomplished tasks, and the way you made others feel welcome and valued in your school community.

▶ REPURPOSE

Current Calendar Use

If you are a digital calendar user, dig into some of the settings and additional tools that allow for a calendar repurposing! Have you spent time looking through settings and features of your calendar? Some features you may find helpful and easy to implement:

- creating tasks and recurring tasks.
- creating custom timelines.
- integrate calendars with your secretary, assistant principal, etc. (knowing you have the ability to click it on only when you need to see those calendars).
- color code types of tasks (i.e., green for observations, blue for meetings, etc.).
- change the view from:
  - daily to see what's up for immediate attention and action.
  - to weekly to capture what you can anticipate may fill your empty blocks.
  - to monthly to get a snapshot of time use for your audit.

▶ REINVEST

"Micro-Moments"

Teachers often use transition times such as lining up or walking to lunch as "teachable moments." Micro-lessons in those little bits of time between instructional sessions, specials, or recess that emphasize skill practice or character building. These moments are often unplanned and determined by what is happening in the context at the moment, yet they can be highly impactful times of extended learning. What if you, as the school leader, used these micro-moments as times to communicate and connect with your staff? As you transition between classes and see teachers in the hall or staff lounge, you can have a predetermined focused message to share with every staff member, or a specific grade or department team. Perhaps you have an email to send to all staff, but really do not want to send out another email. Instead you make a point to use your micro-moments to share that information face-to-face. Micro-moments have the potential to be impactful as your school community can see you are present, available, and approachable. This reinvestment into intentionally timed micro-communication can create stronger relationship bonds and school culture (Vogelgesang, 2025).

Invest, Don't Spend

When we hear the term "invest," our minds may take us first to the area of finance, rather than time use. But we could use finance as an analogy for effective time usage. Consider the 24 hours you have in a day as a bank balance. If your total is only these 24 hours, how much of it do you want to commit to long-term investments, and how much are you willing to spend on the here and now? Investing in your time means that you are allocating time to activities that yield long-term benefits. Whereas time spend is more about immediate tasks. In education, we can probably spend more than 24 hours a day on tasks that are immediate and pressing, but may only solve concerns in the here and now, with little to no payoff for the long term. If we reinvest a portion of our time in tasks that will pay us back in the future, we are being thoughtful and balanced in our time expenditure (Watson, 2018). Consider the tasks you engage in, in your role, that you know for sure have long-term benefits for your staff and students. For example, ensuring collaboration blocks are uninterrupted will benefit the culture and curriculum development as teachers work alongside each other for the betterment of the school. Considering how to balance time investment alongside time spend can assist in tackling both the long-term and short-term demands of your role.

▶ REFINE

Time Blocks

It is time to step away from the traditional thinking about how your time should be spent. We have spent time walking through the time blocking, time chunks, and confetti. Now let us think a little more outside that traditional sense of how we create a schedule. Here we can visit another idea from Levenson and James (2023). They suggest that micro-scheduling can help with focused time during time blocks. This might look like smaller designated blocks within a larger block of time that has been scheduled.

Because many things come up throughout the school day, this may be an effective strategy for staying on top of those pop-ups that infiltrate your day. As a school leader, a 45-minute block of focus time might look like three 15-minute chunks of time set for reviewing and responding to emails, looking at the day's schedule and making updates, and preparing documents and tools for observations. This idea works synergistically with time blocking. Ask yourself:

- Can I envision using micro-scheduling in my day?
- Maybe in the morning, or afternoon, as a starting point for shifting how you use your time?

While we often think about how we schedule our time in larger blocks, we can be more intentional about the smaller chunks to ensure we are meeting our priorities.

> **LINGERING QUESTIONS**
>
> - Have I been approaching my time use thoughtfully, or just reactively and haphazardly?
> - Am I managing my time and schedule or is it managing me?
> - How can I manage my expectations with how I use my time?
> - What strategies will I implement immediately to make better use of my time?
> - How can I build in time for my staff to also evaluate and audit their time use? How will this help them?

In the next chapter, we will get into a highly complex aspect of our school communities: family participation. We get into discussions about the big picture of family involvement and engagement, and the intricacies of how schools currently attempt to engage families. By examining all the moving parts of working with families, we uncover some ways that can help focus on how families can both support school communities and be supported by the school.

References

Brearley, B. (2021, October 24). The cult of busyness. *Thoughtful Leader.* https://www.thoughtfulleader.com/time-management/cult-of-busyness/

Cox, C. (2022). Always in a rush? Maybe it's time urgency. *Psych Central.* https://psychcentral.com/anxiety/always-in-a-rush-maybe-its-time-urgency

Davies, J. (2024). Time management tips for school leaders. *Edutopia.* https://www.edutopia.org/article/time-management-school-leaders/

Eyal, N. (n.d.a). Productivity mindset: How to stay focused and get more done. *Nir and Far.* https://www.nirandfar.com/productivity-mindset/

Eyal, N. (n.d.b). Control your calendar: The secret to managing your time effectively. *Nir and Far.* https://www.nirandfar.com/control-your-calendar/

Hanson, P. (2024, April 18). *How to minimize the damaging effects of meetings starting late.* SwipedOn Workplace Sign In System. https://www.swipedon.com/blog/how-to-minimize-the-damaging-effects-of-meetings-starting-late

Hoff, D. (2019). Why principals must delegate. *SmartBrief.* https://www.smartbrief.com/original/2019/05/why-principals-must-delegate

Kahneman, D., & Tversky, A. (1979). Prospect theory: An analysis of decision under risk. *Econometrica, 47*(2), 263–291.

Knight, J. (2022). *The definitive guide to instructional coaching: Seven factors for success.* ASCD.

Levenson, N., & James, D. (2023). *It's time for strategic scheduling: How to design smarter K–12 schedules that are great for students, staff, and the budget.* ASCD.

McKeown, G. (2021). *Effortless: Make it easier to do what matters most.* Currency.

Meier, J. D. (2010). *Getting results the agile way: A personal system for work and life.* Innovation Playhouse.

Musiowsky-Borneman, T., & Arnold, C. (2021). *The minimalist teacher.* ASCD.

Parker, A. M., Bruine de Bruin, W., & Fischoff, B. (2007). Maximizers versus satisfiers: Decision-making styles, competence, and outcomes. *Judgement and Decision Making, 2*(56), 342–350.

Pink, D. H. (2018). *When: The scientific secrets of perfect timing*. Riverhead Books.

Ross, S. (2025, January 11). The neuroscience of achieving more: Neuroscience-backed time blocking. *Sana Ross*. https://www.sanaross.com/the-neuroscience-of-achieving-more/neuroscience-backed-time-blocking

Rovelli, C. (2018). *The order of time*. Riverhead Books.

Sutton, R. I., & Rao, H. (2024). *The friction project: How smart leaders make the right things easier and the wrong things harder*. St. Martin's Press.

Vogelgesang, K. (2025, February 1). *The power of micro-moments: Transforming lives through small acts of connection*. Scanlan Center for School Mental Health. https://scsmh.education.uiowa.edu/news/2025/02/power-micro-moments-transforming-lives-through-small-acts-connection

Watson, A. (2018, May 13). *What would life look like if you valued your time as much as you value your money?* [Audio podcast episode]. *Truth for Teachers*. https://truthforteachers.com/truth-for-teachers-podcast/value-your-time-as-much-as-you-value-money/

Chapter 6: Editing Family Participation

Family participation often needs a lot of TLC to make it successful, and it needs to be on the priority list because we know that student achievement hinges upon it. Without your families, the school does not exist. Without a working relationship, your community will not thrive. Nurturing relationships and focusing on analogous aspirations for students will result in a prosperous school culture and community (Table 6.1).

Table 6.1 Summary of the 5R's of Editing Family Participation

5R's	Editing Strategies
Reimagine	The role of parents in the school community
Remove	Roadblocks Confusion
Repurpose	School events
Reinvest	Prepare to engage
Refine	The when, why, and what Policies and procedures

DOI: 10.4324/9781003566724-7

▶ FIRST TEACHER

Parents are a child's first teacher. From their entrance into this world, children learn foundational life skills from their parents and caregivers, and often their extended families. They learn how to communicate and how to behave. They learn what is important to them and how to regulate emotions through interactions with their parents. These early experiences shape brain development, cognitive abilities, and social-emotional growth. This is the groundwork for lifelong learning.

Research by Betty Hart, professor of Human Development at the University of Kansas, and Todd Risley, professor in the Department of Psychology at the University of Alaska Anchorage (1995) tell us that children from language-rich home environments hear millions more words by age three than those from less language-focused households. Many early literacy and numeracy skills are developed in established family structures and relationships, as well as their physical health, social/emotional skills, and cultural development (Yang et al., 2021). Pairing this with the knowledge that 90% of brain development occurs by age five (Center on the Developing Child at Harvard University, 2007) should prompt educators to acknowledge the meaningful role parents play in supporting this foundational growth of their child's development. Early experiences with parents and caregivers significantly influence and impact a child's neural connections, shaping a child's capacity for learning, social skills, and emotional resilience.

Recognizing that learning does not just begin when school commences is a ground level assertion that we all need to begin with. Our students come to school with a wealth of knowledge and experiences. Teachers throughout a child's education need to work alongside and build on the foundation that was built in those early years.

▶ THE FAMILY'S ROLE IN STUDENT SUCCESS

The research supporting family engagement's role in student success is clear. Family involvement in school is directly correlated to positive student achievement (Youth.gov, n.d.). John Hattie's (2019) research shows that the effect size of family involvement is 0.45, which is categorized as "having the potential to accelerate student achievement." Dr. Karen Mapp et al.'s (2022) summary of findings showed that these benefits not only the students themselves, but also teachers, families, and entire districts. Districts benefit from improved family involvement systems and the transformation that can occur when families are fully engaged. Higher graduation rates and greater mental health are also reported as a result of involved families. Families report feelings of self-efficacy and the development of leadership skills, and comparatively, teachers tend to remain at schools longer when there is a significant amount of involvement. This involvement indicates that trust between homes and schools has been built and nurtured. In 2023, the United States Department of Education emphasized the importance of home-school partnerships, highlighting collaboration among families, schools, communities, and service providers as essential assets in improving learner outcomes (Schmidt, 2024). This teamwork yields several benefits:

- Increased school participation: Supportive environments enhance attendance, homework completion, and involvement in school activities, which boost student outcomes and achievement.
- Greater self-confidence: Learners and families develop confidence through aligned strategies which foster positive interactions with educators and improve teacher satisfaction.
- Improved academic achievement: Engaged students perform better academically, are more likely to graduate, and maintain consistent attendance and classwork completion.
- Efficient use of resources: Shared decision-making ensures resources are optimized, reducing fragmentation, expanding support services, and enhancing skill acquisition.
- Reduced high-risk behavior: Comprehensive support decreases frustration and disciplinary issues, promoting a positive school climate for all school community members.

Collaboration enhances outcomes for all members of the school community, creating a cohesive and effective learning ecosystem. These efforts invite parents and caregivers to share their cultures, strengths, and love for their children.

The Community as an Ecosystem

A school community can be thought of as its own ecological system (Smith et al., 2023) as it is composed of families, the school, and the broader community. This interactive ecological system influences children's overall well-being and development. In this ecological systems theory, multiple participants are needed to effectively support students in their growth and development. All parts play an important role in the effectiveness of the ecosystem. Similarly to how a missing element in a natural ecosystem will lead to disruptions, so will a missing element in a school ecosystem. The full impact of this is realized through constructive and trusting relationships between educators and families. Building and nurturing the trust with families requires clear, consistent, and supportive communication, as we discussed in our "Editing Communications" chapter. This was reiterated in an American Psychological Association study (Stanford, 2023), supporting the claim that engagements between home and school result in more positive relationships because of the "positive impact on students' social and emotional skills, while decreasing instances of delinquency" (Stanford, 2023, para. 12).

Antony-Newman (2024) boils down the essential elements of family engagement into three critical parts: building relationships, supporting communication, and establishment of partnerships. These three key elements encompass the foundation of what is needed to establish effective family engagement. We have built relationships when we have built trust. Supporting communication means we have tackled the complexities of reaching our specific community in a way that supports their needs. Establishing partnerships entails the recognition of the important role of all individuals involved. These three pillars are needed if we are striving toward family engagement. With this focus, we can stay clear on our purpose with engaging families.

Over several years, Dr. Rebecca Winthrop (2022) was involved in surveying more than 30,000 families and teachers around the world. The survey indicates that all families, regardless of country, language, culture, or economic status, want to be more involved in their children's education. And yet, many working in education would report instances of families not participating or being unresponsive to school activities. Have you experienced low turnout at parent events, school occasions, or community surveys? We need to thoughtfully consider where this discrepancy is coming from. How can we narrow the gap between what families wish for, what we know is effective, and what we are actually seeing?

▶ CAUSE FOR CONCERN

There are many possible causes for reduced or negative family involvement in education. These causes could look and sound like language or cultural barriers, lack of trust, or not feeling they have a place or role in the school community. For example, parents and caregivers may have had negative experiences in their own education and have a hard time trusting the information or sentiments coming from administrators or school staff. There may be families in your community who cannot access school messaging in English and are therefore prevented from full participation. Some families hold a traditional narrative about the "school-as-expert," resulting in a feeling of an imbalance of power or knowledge (Dugan, 2022). Families from different Asian cultures and countries will often send their children to school, or extra classes, for long hours during the day, evenings, and weekends because high academic achievement is of importance to their families. So while schools and teachers are held in high esteem, families see regular school schedules as inadequate for their needs. Additionally, members of the teaching staff may also inadvertently contribute to these barriers because of unconscious biases, blind spots, or confusion about how they can help.

▶ CHANGES IN PARENTING AND GENERATIONAL CHANGES

In addition to the significant barriers mentioned above, we would be remiss if we did not mention that in recent years there has been increased demands on schools to facilitate greater engagement of disenfranchised or marginalized groups. Having had multiple conversations with school principals over time, in multiple locations, there has been a common thread. Because parents can have such varying needs of the school, it can feel like a challenge to please everyone and meet all their wishes (Cross, personal communications, 2024). Simultaneously, teachers find themselves managing the needs of family groups who present with a higher volume of demands and increased expectations of schools than previous generations of parenting groups (Antony-Newman, 2024). These competing demands can cause confusion about where to focus our efforts. It can be challenging for schools to clearly understand their role in family engagement.

In conversation with teachers at a school in Hawai'i, Tammy learned that parents from the younger generations have different expectations and needs compared to earlier generations. One second-grade teacher mentioned that the parents of some of her students struggled to stop bringing their children's backpacks or materials into the classroom for them (Fajardo, personal communications, 2024). She mentioned that there is a desire for parents to do things for their children despite the fact they have been learning to do so independently since kindergarten. This was an observed change from parenting behavior not too long ago. This can often hinder the teaching of independence and responsibility in the school environment. Alongside changes in parenting behaviors, we may also need to make changes in how we enlist and promote family engagement in our schools.

▶ MEETING DIVERSE NEEDS

Over several years, we have heard from school leaders and teachers that some parents (Rothrock, personal communications, 2024):

- want to know exactly what their children are learning, while others just want the gist.
- focus only on their children's classes, while others compare all the goings-on within and between classes and grade levels with siblings and friends, i.e., comparing things like home learning, newsletters, and report cards.
- want pictures of their children showing what they are doing during the day, while others say there is too much messaging coming from the school.

- understand what is asked of them, while others do not understand all the different kinds of communication and their purpose.
- are eager for opportunities for involvement and engagement, while others are happy to not get involved.
- want to know when all the events are, while others just want to know when they need to send money or lunch for trips.
- do not want to get in the way, while others feel they know a better way to teach.
- do not trust the system, while others are willing to hand over responsibility completely to the school.
- are afraid to ask questions or bring up concerns, while others are willing to make contact on a daily basis.

All of these viewpoints have validity and show that we have diverse perspectives and the capability to build trusting relationships with families. At the same time, there may also be flaws in our messaging and miscommunication of expectations. Perhaps we can help parents understand what can be expected from and of the school, rather than having parents come to the school with a list of what could be reasonable or outlandish expectations. Our goal is to help school leaders stay focused on student support and success regardless of the competing ideals families may have, and keep systems simple and clear.

Principal Martin communicates with parents regularly. They have scheduled newsletters to go out each Friday afternoon to recap the week and let parents know what is coming up. Each parent shared an email address and phone number at the start of the school year to receive communications. Most parents opted in to receive emails, while some opted for a link to go to their mobile phones so they could read it there. Teachers also send weekly blogs to parents to that same email or phone number. The office staff sends school updates about events. There are many lines of communication going out but for some reason, parents are not responding to or showing an interest in the upcoming events. Why is this? Is there too much to keep track of? Do the newsletters have specific calls to action for parents? Is there not enough time for parents and caregivers to put events in their calendars? Is the ask unclear? Let us unpack ways to make it easier for parents and caregivers to get more involved and engaged in their children's schools.

▶ DEFINING ASPECTS OF FAMILY PARTICIPATION

In exploring what experts have to say about how to engage families in the school experience, we find that often the recommendations are for teachers to do more. The onus appears to rest with the teachers to be reaching out more, providing more resources, spending more time getting to know the families, communicating more and in more elaborate ways; spending more time doing x, y, z.

As proponents of a minimalist approach to our work, we have struggled to reconcile with this mindset! Especially when there are so many participants within the education system, it seems inequitable for all the effort to be expended only by our already burdened teachers and school administrators. Instead of doing more, more, more, let us have a look at defining what works and refining what we already do to streamline our approach so we can finally see what approaches we can let go of that are not serving our needs.

Involvement versus Engagement

An excellent place to start is to examine the crucial differences between family involvement and family engagement. While they may seem to be synonyms, confidently knowing the difference between the two may support us in making strides forward in a manageable way. Creating a common understanding of what engagement is can support families in understanding how they can shift from being involved to becoming engaged, if that is in their realm of interest. By co-creating or allowing caregivers to engage in this process, we remove this responsibility from school leaders and teachers, and it becomes more about two-way communication and less about information dissemination.

When families are *involved* in school, this is usually done within the control and confines of what the school has decided. Families are invited in for events, celebrations, or offerings. They can choose to attend within the bounds of what the school has determined. Usually the school has initiated this involvement, whereas *engagement* refers to actions and events where families have some ownership over what takes place. They may help make decisions, offer their input, and help frame learning beyond the confines of the classroom. The engagement is mutual, interactive, and shares responsibility.

One way to look at the difference between the two could be in the outcomes of both. While the outcomes of both approaches are potentially positive for culture and relationships, parental engagement with learning is more positively linked to student achievement (Barker & Harris, 2020).

Another significant difference could be boiled down to the family's positioning within the school community. Mapp et al. (2022) define family engagement as "a full, equal and equitable partnership among families, educators and community partners to promote children's learning and development, from birth through college and career" (p. 16). "Family engagement is a strategy that is embedded throughout the work and culture of your school" (Davis, personal communication, 2025), and this changes how the involvement of families is planned, perceived, and received. Are families welcomed and cherished guests in our schools; invited to participate in events, and receive information or guidance? Are they empowered as valuable partners who actively contribute to the educational experiences of the students? This key point can result in whether we are working to *involve* or *engage* the families in our communities.

In Table 6.2, we will examine some of the ways family involvement may present differently to family engagement in common events in school calendars.

School Leadership's Role

As with other topics that we have covered so far in this book, school leaders have a unique role in the approach to family engagement of a school, and to its success. The crucial role that school leaders play will be defined by the tone they set in this arena, the school policies that are created under their watch, the level of involvement that families have, and whether or not they keep abreast of and disseminate the latest research into family engagement in schools. These factors will be greatly influenced by each leader's own experiences, their beliefs, and their understanding of the role of family engagement.

Table 6.2 Opportunities and Occasions for Family Involvement and Engagement

Opportunities and Occasions	Family INVOLVEMENT (School-Directed)	Family ENGAGEMENT (Partnered-Approach)
Back-to-school night	Parents are invited to school and listen to prepared speech from teachers	Parents help plan literacy/math nights where they are actively engaged in the types of learning the students are involved in
Weekly newsletters	One-way communication to disseminate the learning at school	Two-way communication is open between families and school. Opportunities are explored for how learning can be enhanced at home
Reporting	Reports written by teachers and sent home to families on an agreed date	School seeks parent feedback on the clarity and usefulness of the reporting format, asking for what can be improved
Parent-teacher conferences	Teachers outline strengths and goals for students. Parents must attend and have a few moments at the end to ask questions	Two-way dialogue to ascertain strengths and paths forward for the benefit of the student. All parties agree on steps to move forward
Portfolios	Teachers and students prepare portfolios. These are shared with families to review and comment on	Portfolios include family artifacts, aligning learning across contexts. Parent feedback and reflections are included as a part of the portfolio

(Continued)

Table 6.2 Opportunities and Occasions for Family Involvement and Engagement *(Continued)*

Opportunities and Occasions	Family INVOLVEMENT (School-Directed)	Family ENGAGEMENT (Partnered-Approach)
Fundraising events	School decides what the fundraising is for and how it will be carried out. Families are invited to support in predetermined ways	Parent groups have the capability to make decisions around goals, formats, and participation in fundraising types and events themselves
Home "work" and home learning	Homework is assigned and marked by school staff. Parents can see and support the completion of homework	Home learning that is interactive, collaborative, and flexible; designed in a way that does not add stress to the family unit

Smith et al. (2021) found in their research a correlation between principals exhibiting collegial leadership skills and improved family engagement in schools. Interestingly, they found that friendliness and approachability with families were not the main reason why this correlation may occur. Rather, their findings suggest that collegial leadership skills when working with *teachers* may in fact be more impactful. "Several aspects of collegial leadership in particular were found to be significantly associated with family engagement, including when the principal lets teachers know what is expected, sets definite standards of performance, and conducts meaningful evaluation" (p. 10). Perhaps then, a school culture of understanding and trust among faculty will lead to teachers engaging more and more positively with families.

Hiring practices can also be an important facet of meeting family needs. Family units are unique and while we can generalize needs, there will often be specific demands that require extra attention. Staff members who speak more than one language could be advantageous for the whole community (St. Augustine College, 2024). In hiring practices, it might be worth posting positions that request, not require, staff to speak a second language. Having multilingual staff who can speak the language of families may assist them to feel included and valued. While many schools have ways to translate materials, a speaker is always helpful when there are questions and clarifications to be made.

Ms. Landes had been principal of her middle school for several years and over her tenure, the family demographics started changing about three years in. New families were moving in from different French-speaking countries. Because of this change in demographic, Ms. Landes knew she needed to respond to the change. She needed to hire staff for a few open positions and on the postings, she included the interest in having French-speakers apply as a resource to French-speaking families.

Tiered Family Engagement

Have you and your staff considered how a differentiated approach to teaching and learning is a required expectation, and yet, our approach to family engagement is often a one-size-fits-all approach? The way in which we deal with family engagement is frequently a universal approach – everyone will get the same information, at the same time and the same opportunities to engage with their child's education. When we are aware that our students will have varying needs in their educational experience, we must also recognize that their families may require varying responses and support in their experience with our schools. Bachman and Boone (2022) have argued for a multi-tiered response to improving family engagement. They outline a flexible, responsive approach to engagement and support across three tiers: universal, tailored, and intensive. Rather than labeling families according to tiers, they suggest that school administrators proactively plan ahead for tiered supports, resources, and practices that allow for differentiated engagement when needed. This way, schools can avoid reactively responding when the universal engagement options fail for some families.

Let us look at a few examples of this multi-tiered system:

- Universal tier – This tier provides broad, inclusive strategies to engage all families and caregivers, creating a

welcoming school culture to ensure access to general resources. These might include:
- Hosting school-wide events such as open houses, family literacy nights, or cultural celebrations to foster a sense of community and inclusivity.
- Regularly distributing newsletters or like communication through multiple, appropriate channels (emails, apps, printed flyers) to keep families informed about school activities, curriculum, and events.

- Tailored tier – This tier involves differentiated strategies to meet the needs of specific subsets of families and caregivers based on shared characteristics or challenges. This might include:
  - Providing translated materials or multilingual parent workshops for families with limited English proficiency to support their understanding of school processes and resources.
  - Organizing workshops or support groups for families with students who have special or specified needs, offering targeted resources and strategies.
  - Sending specific messages to caregivers via services like Remind or portfolio programs like Seesaw.
- Intensive tier – This tier focuses on specialized support for families who require more personalized interventions. This might include:
  - Conducting home visits to build trust and provide direct support for families facing significant barriers to engagement, such as transportation or economic challenges.
  - Partnering with community organizations to provide services such as mental health counseling or housing assistance to address acute family needs impacting student success.

This tiered model ensures that engagement efforts are broad for the whole community, yet inclusive, responsive, and adaptable to the diverse and varying needs of families in the school community. As always, planning for all supports initially saves us time and effort in reacting or repairing at a later date.

Bring Home to School versus School to Home

Effective collaboration between home and school is crucial for enhancing student outcomes. The terms "Bring Home-to-School" and "School-to-Home" refer to the direction of engagement efforts (Levy, 2023). School-to-Home means extending school learning and expectations into the home setting, whereas Home-to-School involves integrating family insights, values, and cultural backgrounds into the school ecosystem.

Families often experience bringing school-to-home versus the home-to-school. Mass amounts of what we hope is important schoolwide communications often dictate this directionality, and we do not as often seek the inverse. When we focus in this way, we are dictating what the interaction and relationship mean and look like for families, and that may not meet their needs. What we mean here is that bringing Home-to-School more often, more efficiently, and effectively allows a space for caregivers and the school staff to be truly collaborative in their efforts to create a strong and streamlined school culture for all its constituents.

A common literacy practice in Ms. Ashton's junior school in Australia was to start the week with a journal writing practice. The young students at her school would retell the events of their weekends while refining their writing skills. As she visited classrooms each Monday morning, she started noticing patterns in the content of her students' journal entries. Throughout the winter, her students wrote about their weekend practices and games of Australian Rules Football. Ms. Ashton realized that this commonality in weekend activities offered an opportunity to engage families with school. She invited parents, who were also football coaches, to offer workshops for all the students and staff, and other parents to facilitate and join in. These sessions created enjoyable engagement for the whole school community to communicate, collaborate, and be active together. By utilizing this common ground and popular cultural activity, the school community was able to build relationships and move forward together with a positive and respectful approach with each other.

Asset-Based Approach versus Deficit Approach

One consideration to reflect on is whether we are perceiving family engagement from an asset-based approach or a deficit-based approach. A deficit-based approach is one in which the school is seen as needing to identify problems, solve these problems, or meet a need that is lacking. This approach frames the school staff as the holders of knowledge and requires them to seek out the gaps or issues and assist caregivers to do a better job. Whereas an asset-based approach utilizes the strengths that caregivers already possess to ensure school success. This mindset considers caregivers as partners and collaborators, and encourages school staff to adapt, rather than simply expect.

Knowing where our mindset and methodology currently lie is important in navigating a path forward. Once your current status is recognized, you can then decide on what you want your future approach to be and plot a path to making that a reality. It is important to note that our path forward may not need to be either-or. It is possible that a fluid approach could be used to meet the changing needs and attitudes of community members. It might be necessary to share knowledge at times, but to harness the strengths of the community at others.

THE 5R's: EDITING STRATEGIES FOR FAMILY PARTICIPATION

▶ REIMAGINE

Role of Parents in Your Community

The role that teachers, students, and families play in learning and engagement can be reimagined when teachers and administrators let go of more traditional ideas about the parts we play. We can see from the discussion above that the role of families and caregivers is important and can impact student experiences. We recognize the mindset we hold about the role they play will impact how we work alongside our community members. We are aware that different members of the community may need different types of support at different times. We also acknowledge the varied strengths that our families bring to our communities. So it is important that we reimagine the roles of caregivers from what may traditionally have been thought of.

In their book, *In Search of Deeper Learning: The Quest to Remake the American High School* (2019), Jal Metha and Sarah Fine stated that "[g]rounded institutions celebrate the diversity of communities by connecting with families to create a unique educational experience, rather than expecting them to assimilate into existing school norms" (p. 90). The uniqueness of families allows for an asset-based view of family engagement. Reinvest the time in getting to know diverse perspectives and experiences of families and realize that not all family involvement will look the same.

How can everyone have a more equitable part to play? Explore different opportunities in your context where you could leverage the assets of your community. The school communications and relationships can serve as the springboard for parents to take ownership of requests and commitments to their children. Different members of the community can utilize their strengths, experience, and areas of interest in order to work for the benefit of the student body.

Let us look at what this can look like in your school (Table 6.3).

Table 6.3 Role of Parents in the School Community

Who	Asset	What	How
Mr. Sampson, ES Parent	Mr. Sampson is a writer and avid reader. He has worked for many years in the local library.	Volunteers in the school library and helps organize the school Book Week activities.	Mr. Sampson has set aside a few hours a week to work alongside the School Librarian helping to reshelve books, check out books, or advise on the management systems. Once a year he collaborates with teachers to arrange Book Week.

(Continued)

Table 6.3 Role of Parents in the School Community *(Continued)*

Who	Asset	What	How
Ms. Channing, MS Parent	Ms. Channing is a logistics coordinator who enjoys working with technology.	Coordinates guest speakers for monthly student assemblies.	Keeps a shared document with a table listing the speaker's name, connection to the assembly theme, and date of guest. Adds speakers to the school Google calendar.
Mr. Kasinski, HS Parent	Mr. Kasinski loved Science when he was a student and won two prizes at the Science Fair.	Helps HS Science teachers prepare lab materials.	HS Science teachers share their timetables with Mr. Kasinski so he can plan out when he can come in to prepare materials by leaving them in labeled baskets on the side shelf.

▶ REMOVE

Roadblocks and Barriers

Remove roadblocks that may be literally or figuratively preventing more active involvement and engagement. Just remove them! Sounds like an easy task, but we know it requires thinking through and planning. Roadblocks such as knowledge gaps, language, or unexplained cultural norms can make caregivers feel incompetent or not valued. Whenever requests to parents go out, review them with your team to ensure that all messaging is clear and make accommodations for specific families. Create a spreadsheet with a list of the families, the potential roadblocks you know specific families may experience, and add a column for the potential solutions or strategies for the roadblock removal, even if that list is long. Wherever you can, ask for feedback about how things are going. Be more specific with your feedback requests than just enjoyment. Ask families to rate the timing, approach, and accessibility of the various engagement opportunities offered.

We love an audit to evaluate systems and effectiveness so it makes sense that we suggest auditing the barriers that exist within your school community. What are the items that are barriers for your specific family community? Make a simple list and create an action step for each barrier.

Level: Primary/elementary

- Barrier: Limited availability due to work schedules.
- Action Step: Record short videos of meetings to recap information.
- Resources: Digital spaces.

Level: Middle school

- Barrier: Communication breakdown between school, parents, and students.
- Action Step: Create a system for student-led check-in and communications with school and parents.
- Resources: Digital spaces.

Level: High school

- Barrier: Lack of parent confidence in supporting academics.
- Action Step: Offer parent workshops for supporting students at high school academic levels.
- Resources: Resource guides.

Confusion

While we can think of confusion as a barrier as well, we are going to single it out here. Perhaps we can extend another idea from the educational philosophy of Winthrop. Winthrop (2022) stated that there is an importance in making space for intentional conversations about the purpose of school – and here we will say parent involvement. What we need is an element from a classic model of good instruction. Parents need examples (and maybe nonexamples) of what involvement is and can be, beyond a definition. Even before we tell or instruct parents on "here's what YOU need to do as a parent," let us step back and look at the big picture first.

1. Share data from schools with high involvement versus low involvement, from all levels.
2. Share examples of what the involvement from parents looked like at these successful schools.
3. Co-create a definition of what involvement means and provide examples of what it looks like.
4. Co-create a definition of what engagement means and provide examples of what it looks like.
5. Have parents identify what is in their sphere of interest and they can manage with their other responsibilities.
6. Create a plan and calendar for who, what, when, and where that involvement and engagement looks like in people's lives.
7. Create an accountability check-in process to ensure that everyone takes on the ownership for what they agreed to.
8. Communicate the plan, calendar, and accountability process to the school community through your communication channels.
9. Survey parents, staff, and students regarding how the involvement of parents is working, and ask for feedback.
10. Celebrate the successes.

This kind of step-by-step can remove the confusion that was festering with parents, and potentially even staff. With clear and focused steps, your community can move toward stronger parent and guardian communication and involvement.

▶ REPURPOSE

School Events

In contemplating the priorities and importance of family participation, you may be rethinking the yearly events that come up in your own school calendar. A complete overhaul of already existing events may not be necessary. But rather, a repurposing through a new lens. Your school may well have traditional events that the community looks forward to each year that could use some small tweaks in order to make them more purposeful and meaningful. Use this invigoration of the importance of family engagement to retool existing events. This can create a greater impact on relationship building and culture. Let us examine some standard school events:

- Parent-teacher conferences: Work with your team to consider how you could elevate this to leverage engagement, family assets, and voice.
- Curriculum evening: Refocuses on two-way dialogue, rather than a dissemination of information.
- Graduation ceremonies: Explore potential barriers to understanding or participation from your community.
- Back-to-School night: Examine how this event could be reworked to consider the multi-tiered needs of different families.

Take your time to shift one expected event one by one, remembering that change does not happen overnight, and requires reflection and revision. Small incremental changes in a thoughtful direction will enable sustainable change for the betterment of the school culture and community.

▶ REINVEST

Prepare to Engage!

We can see from this discussion that family engagement has a crucial role in the work that we do for students. Positive family/school connections can significantly impact the educational experience of our students. But how prepared are we to pave this important pathway as educators? From the beginning of our career to becoming veterans in the field, how much training, investment, and time is spent in identifying and promoting the important role that these partnerships have?

Studies into teacher preparation programs indicate that little or no time is put into how and why we need to develop family partnerships, leaving educators feeling unprepared (de Bruïne et al., 2014). University courses may have no formal inclusion of this area of education, leaving teachers to learn how to navigate partnerships on their own. Educators' personality, opinions, and personal experiences will undoubtedly then have an impact on how we perceive our role with families. And, our early experiences working in education could potentially also drastically impact our view moving forward in our careers.

Schools need to carefully consider this and ensure they are investing adequate time into how they train, discuss, and mentor their teachers to support their vision of family participation. Our policies and guidelines need to be clearly stated to ensure we are all working in the same way with this. Consideration should be given to including dedicated sessions in our professional development plans. Coaching has been found to be an effective way to support educators in this area, as has engaging in activities such as family nights, with families and educators sharing and communicating together (Paul et al., 2023). Family involvement events could have the potential to build trust and relationships, as well as educator confidence to work alongside caregivers. Ongoing coaching could provide support and assistance over time to build awareness, skills, and self-efficacy in the work we do.

▶ REFINE

The When, Why, and What of Family Participation

We have mentioned above that it is likely that your school already has participation events scheduled throughout the school year. A thoughtful review of when these happen, how often they take place, what the topic is, and why we are doing them will be helpful to ensure you are editing your practices effectively. Here, the key thing to remember is to engage early, positively, and often.

When Micha started the fourth grade, her parents attended the back-to-school night at the beginning of the year. Following that, Micha's parents' next point of contact with the school was the first report card of the year. They were alarmed to find out that not only was she struggling in reading, but was also being disruptive in class. They contacted Ms. Yang, the teacher, and arranged for a meeting. They were disappointed with the conversation they had with Ms. Yang and left feeling unheard, confused about the school's approach, and concerned about Micha's lack of achievement in her class. They were not sure how to help Micha, but were reluctant to sit down with Ms. Yang again. Instead they decided to wait to speak with her fifth-grade teacher when the following year started.

Ms. Yang, on the other hand, was following the school event calendar and assumed that Micha's parents understood the expectations and barriers she faced. Ms. Yang was disappointed in the lack of engagement and participation from Micha's parents. She did what she could to support Micha in class, but felt that it would be limited in its effectiveness without a supportive home environment. If there had been more opportunities in the school year for Ms. Yang, Micha, and her parents to connect, communicate, and build a relationship, how could this situation have changed?

Frequent opportunities to work together, that begin early in the year, allow schools and families to build effective, collaborative partnerships. Positive dialogue and tone can be formative in engaging parents. Involving parents early and often can build networks and a sense of belonging (Barker & Harris, 2020). While there may be no one-size-fits-all approach to successful family participation, the notion of engaging early and often will be helpful and transformative.

It will also be advantageous to consider the changing needs of family participation across a students' school career. In the early years, close collaboration with a focus on sharing activities that support development is beneficial. As students move into elementary school, families can participate more in events like field trips, assemblies, and fairs, while also learning about the curriculum and strategies to assist learning. And while our middle school and high school students begin wanting (and needing!) more autonomy and independence, parent attendance at school events will still convey a message about the importance of education. In addition to that, our older students benefit from engaging in meaningful conversations that connect the complex topics they are learning about to the real world (Australian Institute for Teaching and School Leadership, 2024).

Keeping simple systems for families so that they want to engage and see the benefit of their engagement will support not only their child's journey through school, but also help to create a positive and caring school community. Educators at all levels need to be prepared to engage with families in authentic ways to create and maintain a strong, positive, and fulfilling relationship between the school and home. Ultimately, "(f)amily engagement pathways must begin early, persist across time, and transform according to age and context" (Barker & Harris, 2020).

Policies and Procedures

School policies and procedures that highlight the active role that families could play will not only help parents and caregivers understand their role, but also that they are valuable members of the community. There is no school without their children, after all. Clear policies and procedures also give staff the guidelines for how to engage with parents and offer support for gaining their involvement. As mentioned earlier in the book, the written artifacts of our schools are an essential way to state and evidence what and why we are operating in the ways that we do. Using the strategies suggested in this chapter, carefully think through a refining of the policies and procedures to include the following:

- Hiring practices that incorporate consideration of family engagement.
- Professional development plans that include attention to family engagement.
- Alignment between family engagement practices and the school's vision and values.
- A pre-planned and articulated path to a multi-tiered approach to family engagement.
- Intentionally planned and articulated approach to bring school to home, and home to school.

LINGERING QUESTIONS

- How can an audit help us examine what family involvement and engagement look like at our school?
- What are the barriers we can address quickly, and which will take more time to tackle?
- What are the assets our families bring to our community?

We have spent a substantial portion of the book outlining your role as a leader, the challenges you may encounter, and offered ways to rethink the responsibilities that often weigh you down. In the next chapter, we share ideas focusing on your well-being as an educational leader. We sifted through the unwieldy amount of ideas out there about what well-being could or should be, and found some strong focal points that will support you as a leader. Here we aim to cut to the heart of what you need in your role, and we hope you take time to strategically rethink your well-being plan too.

References

Antony-Newman, M. (2024). Parent engagement and the teaching profession: A policy framework. *School Community Journal, 34*(2), 111–130.

Australian Institute for Teaching and School Leadership. (2024). *Strengthening parent engagement to improve student outcomes.* https://www.aitsl.edu.au/research/spotlights/strengthening-parent-engagement-to-improve-student-outcomes

Bachman, H. F., & Boone, B. J. (2022). A multi-tiered approach to family engagement. *Educational Leadership, 80*(1), 58–62.

Barker, B., & Harris, D. (2020). Parent and family engagement: An implementation guide for school communities. *Australian Research Alliance for Children and Youth.* https://www.aracy.org.au/wp-content/uploads/2024/09/ARACY-Parent-and-Family-Engagement-Implementation-Guide.pdf

Center on the Developing Child at Harvard University. (2007). *The science of early childhood development: Closing the gap between what we know and what we do.* Harvard University.

de Bruïne, E. J., Willemse, T. M., D'Haem, J., Griswold, P., Vloeberghs, L., & van Eynde, S. (2014). Preparing teacher candidates for family–school partnerships. *European Journal of Teacher Education, 37*(4), 409–425. https://doi.org/10.1080/02619768.2014.912628

Dugan, J. (2022). Co-constructing family engagement. *Educational Leadership, 80*(1). https://www.ascd.org/el/articles/co-constructing-family-engagement

Hart, B., & Risley, T. R. (1995). *Meaningful differences in the everyday experience of young American children.* Paul H. Brookes Publishing.

Hattie, J. (2019). *Visible learning: A synthesis of over 800 meta-analyses relating to achievement.* Routledge.

Levy, R. (2023). Home–school communication: What we have learned from the pandemic. *Education 3-13, 52*(1), 21–32. https://doi.org/10.1080/03004279.2023.2186972

Mapp, K. L., Henderson, A. T., Cuevas, S., Franco, M. C., & Ewert, S. (2022). *Everyone wins! The evidence for family-school partnerships and implications for practice.* Scholastic.

Mehta, J., & Fine, S. (2019). *In search of deeper learning: The quest to remake the American high school.* Harvard University Press.

Paul, J., Sudduth, M., Woodard, M., Pruitt, C., & Hill, K. (2023). Empowering pre-service educators to build multilingual spaces through family engagement. *The Reading Paradigm, 16*(1), 16–22.

Schmidt, J. (2024, September 30). The importance of home & school collaboration when developing daily living skills. *Life Skills Advocate.* https://lifeskillsadvocate.com/blog/the-importance-of-home-school-collaboration-when-developing-daily-living-skills/

Smith, J., Johnson, R., & Lee, A. (2023, July). Does parent involvement really help students? Here's what the research says. *Education Week.* https://www.edweek.org/leadership/does-parent-involvement-really-help-students-heres-what-the-research-says/2023/07

Smith, T. E., Reinke, W. M., Herman, K. C., & Sebastian, J. (2021). Exploring the link between principal leadership and family engagement across elementary and middle school. *Journal of School Psychology, 84,* 49–62.

St. Augustine College. (2024, May 2). The benefits of being bilingual in the workplace. https://www.staugustine.edu/2024/05/02/benefits-of-being-bilingual-in-the-workplace/

Stanford, L. (2023, July 10). Does parent involvement really help students? Here's what the research says. *Education Week.*

Winthrop. (2022, June 27). *How to build collaborative relationships between families and schools.* Teacher Magazine. https://www.teachermagazine.com/au_en/articles/how-to-build-collaborative-relationships-between-families-and-schools

Yang, Q., Yang, J., Zheng, L., Song, W., & Yi, L. (2021). Impact of home parenting environment on cognitive and psychomotor development in children under 5 years old: A meta-analysis. *Frontiers in Pediatrics, 9,* 658094. https://doi.org/10.3389/fped.2021.658094

Youth.gov. (n.d.). *Impact of family engagement.* https://youth.gov/youth-topics/impact-family-engagement

Chapter 7
Remedy Your Well-Being

There is no time better than this moment to focus on you. Perhaps the last thing you want to read more about is well-being. Well, stay for a few moments because we would like to bring some potentially new ideas and research about well-being we would like you to think through. You may notice the summary of the 5R's shows no mention of the spa or "Me Time." While we support these short-term actions to give yourself some space to relax, we ask you to think more deeply about well-being, the impact it has on your work, your family, and other areas of your life (Table 7.1).

Table 7.1 The 5R's for Remedying Leader Well-Being

5R's	Editing Strategies
Reimagine	The power of positive emotions
Remove	The concept of well-being as an individual responsibility
	The stigma
Repurpose	Our tired notions of self-care
Reinvest	Time and effort in building relationships
Refine	Your movement
	Your relationship with sleep

▶ WORTHY CONSIDERATION, OR A NON-ISSUE?

You may have noticed that most of the contents of this book were focused on what the leader does in the school day. We have purposefully not addressed the home life of a school leader, yet we know and cannot ignore the reality that school leaders take their work home with them physically, mentally, and emotionally. We know that the personal lives of leaders become sort of a public domain as so many school community members "need" the attention of the school leaders. On the other hand, leaders in education generally have healthy salaries, comfortable offices, autonomy to make decisions, and plenty of staff to delegate to. So of course they are all thriving, right? And therefore it is okay that the lives of school leaders are front and center of praise and criticism at any time, *right*?

Mounting research is starting to suggest otherwise. Changing expectations and work conditions are leading to increasing challenges for leaders in achieving positive well-being (Beausaert et al., 2021). Principals are reporting far higher levels of stress and stress-related symptoms, such as sleeping problems or depression, than the general population (TES, n.d.). Our school leaders are struggling to maintain self-care habits, particularly in maintaining good sleep habits and exercising regularly. Scrutiny and criticism take their toll as well, with almost half of school leaders in one survey reporting to have been verbally attacked either in person or online in one year alone (NASSP Survey, 2022). Loneliness for school leaders is frequently a concern, with people holding these positions feeling the loss of external support and a peer group to confide in (Kelly, 2019). School leaders often leave their roles after a short time at their post, and stay in a single position for a shorter time than is optimal for enacting change (Gacherieu, 2024). We know that this turnover can impact the strength of the school community, culture, and entire ecosystem.

As we have seen in previous chapters, our school leaders have a significant role in supporting our schools. Their role has an impact on the culture of the school, student success, parent engagement, and school improvement. There is a direct line between school leader well-being and the well-being of the community as a whole. Ignoring the significant issues around school leader well-being is ignoring an impact factor for the success of the school and its community members.

We believe it is a worthy consideration to come back to Schein's three levels of expectations, applying it here to well-being (Geraghty, n.d.). What are the artifacts, espoused values, and underlying assumptions that are evident regarding leader well-being?

- Artifacts:
  - There may be artifacts of your well-being strategies and plans present, or there may be few. Review your school policies or job description for any existing information about well-being expectations.
- Espoused values:
  - Think about the beliefs you hold about discovering, strengthening, or recovering your well-being practices. Do they align with your actions? Here is when we want to ensure we are "walking the walk." If you are encouraging a colleague to schedule some downtime, you should be doing the same.
- Underlying assumptions:
  - There may be some underlying assumptions and strongly held beliefs that leaders are not able to make their well-being a priority because of the magnitude of the role. We should not assume this. There are educational leaders who have been strategic and intentional about focusing on their well-being. Some of these leaders document their well-being journeys for us to witness on social media. We can use these as a source for learning and inspiration. You can debunk the underlying assumptions about school leader well-being through your actions and support for others.

The Leadership Mask

One factor that may be contributing to the impact on school leader well-being is the often felt need to keep a professional front on at all times. Kelly (2023) calls this the "Leadership Mask." Despite carrying a significant amount of emotional burden or labor, those in leadership positions may feel the need to display a consistent professional, stoic facade, devoid of an extreme range of emotional reactions. There are many emotional demands placed on school leaders that can eventuate in levels of stress and tiredness that may not be present in other professions. Leaders deal with different individuals or groups of people with competing demands, needs, and expectations, coupled with long working hours. They have chosen a caring profession and may struggle with compassion fatigue. Their concern for their community may result in ongoing worry into evenings, weekends, and holidays. Simultaneously, they may also feel the need to maintain the appearance of professionalism. This may require hiding their own feelings, expressing feelings they may not actually be having, or placing their own emotions to the side while working to support others. Leaders may be striving to hide their perceived vulnerabilities or uncertainty about the best way to proceed.

Wearing the leadership mask may add to the burdens of school leaders as it can disconnect you from who you really are. It may inadvertently disconnect you from others as well, as they sense that you are not being authentically yourself. Not to mention the exhaustion that can come from pretending to be or feel something that you are not.

Despite the toll it may be taking, school leaders may feel that the mask is still a necessary part of the role. Wearing the mask may provide an emotional shield that enables you to move forward, guide others, and perform to the expectations of all those you work with. Simply dropping the leadership mask may not be the best possible solution moving forward in these roles. Leaders may need to think of alternative solutions to make time and space for our authentic selves to experience and deal with the full range of emotions they confront in the course of their work.

Patterns of Stress

The extensive research about the effect of stress and trauma on brain development by neuroscientists, Perry and Hambrick (2008) tell us that there are definite patterns in the stress responses we have in our lives. Dr. Perry's development of the "Neurosequential Model of Therapeutics" tells us that stress patterns can move us into two different response modes. When we experience extreme, unpredictable, and long-term stress, we shift into a dysregulated state, causing us to be "sensitized" by the stressor. On the other hand, when we experience a more healthy and productive stress that is moderate, predictable, and short-lived, we can move into a state of resilience-building, which can be deemed as therapeutic.

If we think about these patterns of stress, we may experience both of them in our roles as school leaders. We would hope that the stress we experience leans into the resilience building, pushing us into problem-solving and challenge-addressing modes, nothing that pushes our stress levels into the high-alert, fight, flight, or freeze mode. The reality is that some of you out there may be experiencing this sensitizing to extreme and unpredictable situations in your setting.

Rita was the principal of an upper elementary school in a large urban environment. Her students were living in poverty situations, lived in homes in which domestic abuse and violence were the norm, and often students exhibited disruptive and sometimes dangerous behaviors. Her work life meant she was living in a sensitizing stress zone. Because parents and students were often coming into the school in a high state of stress that was often hard to predict, Rita was often on edge first thing in the morning, despite her trying to create a calm and welcoming school environment for her staff and students. Over her ten-year tenure at the school, the dynamics shifted because of the focus on emotional regulation strategies and building relationships. Over time, Rita, her staff, and students experienced less of the daily, unpredictable stressors. This shift in patterns of stress allowed them to function in a less high-alert manner.

Micro-Stressors; Mega-Problems

We can all recognize the stress that comes along with serious, significant events and issues that arise in schools. Whether it is navigating through a pandemic, dealing with violence, or a weather crisis for community members, we can all readily acknowledge how challenging these moments can be. You may have attended a session or course on crisis management as part of your professional development over the years.

But one hardship that we may not be able to easily see is the cumulative effect of many ongoing stressors over a longer period of time. These microstressors, made up of smaller, nagging, or irritating events or interactions, can have a much more significant impact on our well-being than we might realize. This might not be something you have been trained to deal with, or even considered as an issue. Ongoing or persistent frustrations may actually be a more accurate predictor of mental and physical health than a one-off major life event (Boardman, 2021).

Picture this: you went for a refill of coffee, only to find the coffee pot empty. Then you head to the photocopier, only to find it jammed from the previous user. On your knees trying to pull that crumpled paper out, a teacher asks you for a due date on that feedback (which you know was in this morning's announcements). Finally returning to your computer, you see an email from a parent lodging a new complaint with you. Each individual event is not anything drastic or unexpected, and all are manageable. However, the person who next pops their head around the corner to ask a question may get a different response than if there had been plentiful coffee and a dependable photocopier! Or, if you had had a few more minutes to reset after these events. Accruing these minor annoyances can impact our well-being and how we carry ourselves through the day. Recognizing the impact of amassed micro-stressors and working to lessen their impact is an important consideration in school leaders' well-being.

Let's Not Remember Our Why

A message we often hear and revisit, especially in recent years in education, in professional learning sessions, and maybe even at our faculty meetings is to "remember your why."

> Remember why you got into this field.
> Remember what is really important in this work we do.
> Remember your purpose.

For some of us, this is a reminder we need to stay motivated and keep doing the hard work we do. *Don't get caught up in the little challenges or annoyances. Don't let petty irritations derail you from the positives.* Instead, focus on the big picture. The world around you may be trying to divert your attention away from what you do. *Don't let it.* Refocus on what is important for you.

For others, this is a glib statement. It is a throwaway sentence directed at trying to make the best of the situation. Right up there alongside "live, laugh, love" in terms of appeal and audience. This may be THE toxic phrase at the root of many issues in education today. The idea that educators need to become society's doormat while we let the needs and expectations of others walk all over us. Tied up inextricably with toxic positivity, if we can only remember our "why," all other concerns around cost-of-living expenses, untenable workloads, burnout, and unreal expectations will simply fall away. We can realize our truly altruistic, virtuous selves if we just remember why we are doing this challenging and sometimes thankless work. All other issues will simply become irrelevant.

As we know, there is no simple answer to this. It resonates with some, and it does not for others, and that is going to happen with a diverse group of people. Ultimately, if it works for you, then who are we to question it? In truth, peeling back the layers of what minimalism is, getting to the heart of purpose is what it is all about. Through finding a purpose, you can remove the things that do not and are not serving you in working toward that purpose.

The reality for many, though, is that simply remembering our why is not going to be enough to sustain our well-being throughout a career in education. No matter what role is held in education, this work is hard. It has the potential to take a lot from us in terms of our well-being. The effort, the care, the hours spent, the dedication to getting it right, may well take a toll on how we experience our lives.

As our world and expectations shift, so does our understanding of what well-being can and should like. We now have very real data about what can help you feel better in your work and in your day-to-day life. We have this data about what works for humans in general, and about what can work specifically for educators. Can we be so inclined and ask:

- What if we harnessed this information and utilized it to actually make us feel better in the work that we do?
- What could it look like if you and the others around you felt energized and happy throughout your workweek?
- Would we see a reduction in burnout and in those leaving the profession?

▶ DO NOT OVERLOOK WHAT YOU DO AFTER WORK

We have focused a lot in this book on what can be done within schools to edit and simplify what we do in the hopes that we feel better doing our work. It can be hard to examine our lives outside of work, as our contexts and situations can vary so much, and the way in which individuals spend their lives is dependent on so many different factors. While we could ignore this facet of leader well-being, psychology research highlights that this may be a factor that we cannot ignore.

In organizational psychology, there has been a recent increase in interest around how our post-work, or off-job activities, influence our well-being when we are actually at work. This work recovery is aimed at reducing stress or strain back to what it was before triggers, stress reactions, or negative-feeling emotions commenced. This work recovery can only begin when the demands of the work have finished and is usually dependent on the person undergoing some sort of experience or activity unrelated to that work. Evening, weekend, and vacation recovery processes, as well as micro-breaks during the day, can aid motivation, energy levels, and lead to improved well-being (Sonnentag et al., 2022). Physical activities and experiences that assist us to psychologically detach from work are identified as being particularly effective processes.

An interesting point from the above research shows that if the work demands do not stop, or are added to from other sources, the work recovery process does not start. These stressors can also accumulate over time. So if you are contemplating an issue at work while running on a treadmill, you may be receiving the physical benefits of the exercise, but not giving yourself the psychological detachment you need to actually tackle that issue to the best of your abilities. A true break is needed to reset and start fresh again the next day.

Sleep as Fuel

Christine is a crier. She cries at TV shows, movies, books, when someone says something nice, or through frustration. She has cried at music festivals, art galleries, sunrises, and of course, bidding farewell to students on the last day of school. But ever since she was a small child, it was obvious that how tired she was, directly influenced how close she was to tears. Sleep, or lack of sleep, has a huge impact on how well we can manage big emotions and our response to them.

It is for this reason that we cannot move past a discussion about our lives outside of work and well-being without mentioning sleep. Your relationship to sleep may well be one of the most essential elements to reflect on when approaching positive well-being. Ariana Huffington describes sleep as "the fuel for life" in her 2016 book, *The Sleep Revolution: Transforming Your Life, One Night at a Time*. It is what keeps us going, feeling good, helps us see clearly, and get along well with others.

Lacking quality sleep is related to higher chances of cardiovascular disease, stroke, asthma, arthritis, depression, diabetes, and being overweight (McKeown, 2014). Beyond that we know the impact it has on our cognitive faculties, problem-solving skills, and ability to handle stress. We are sure we can all recognize in our own lives that the distance between an issue and a melt down is directly correlated to the amount of sleep we are running on! Or is that just us?!

A survey of more than 2000 Americans in 2014 found that 70% of people respond to stress by sleeping less than they usually do (Harvard School of Public Health, Robert Wood Johnson Foundation, & NPR, 2014). In the same survey respondents reported that getting a full night's sleep was more effective in reducing stress than using prescription medication, receiving professional help, or following a self-help program. So while reduced sleep is a very common response to stress, the exact opposite behavior can be instrumental in feeling better and responding more effectively.

Letting go of narratives such as "I don't need much sleep" and giving sleep the time and attention it deserves may well pay off in many ways in our lives. Rather than delaying or reducing our sleep to get more accomplished, actually getting that good night's rest will help us be better versions of ourselves to get things done later. Tackling our tasks and interactions with a well-rested body and mind will result in more effective, productive, positive, and thoughtful work completion.

A Simpler Way to Well-Being?

Ali Abdaal has attempted to lead us on a path in this work of well-being. In his 2023 book, *Feel Good Productivity*, Abdaal discusses ways we can harness research into well-being in a way that will help us feel good while we get our work done well. Rather than just sacrificing ourselves and our well-being for the sake of our work performance, the author sets out to describe strategies and tools that we could use to enjoy ourselves while also performing at our best. He summarizes this into three main categories: Energi[z]e, Unblock, and Sustain.

- To Energize, Abdaal discusses how we can incorporate a more playful attitude, focus on what we have control over, and enjoy working alongside the people around us.
- To Unblock, Abdaal describes how we find clarity over what is holding us back, while utilizing brain science to hack into ways we can get motivated.
- To Sustain, Abdaal shares ways we can keep this carrying on into the long term, by conserving energy and making sure to recharge ourselves.

While none of this may sound ground breaking, it serves as a potent reminder to us that maybe we do not need to twist ourselves into knots to feel better while doing our work. We know how much better it feels to have good friends at work. We are aware that a day that includes laughter is better than a day that does not. It is not rocket science to understand that being aware of what is stopping us from the work will be more helpful than remaining in denial. We know that one-off attempts at well-being are only a band-aid on possible, larger ongoing issues. We will touch back to the tips from Abdaal when we move into the 5R's section further into the chapter to help us energize, unblock, and sustain.

The Slow Movement

Slow and school do not go together, do they? Well, maybe they should. The "Slow Movement" was introduced as a counter to the increase in the pace of life and the increased availability of fast food in the 1980s (Blankson, 2022). This increased pace of everything has not been to our benefit in the long term.

In one episode of our podcast, *The Minimalist Educator* (2024), we discuss the intent of bringing the idea of slowing down into schools (episode 53). Doing everything at high rates of speed reduces the quality of our work because of the limited attention we give to our tasks and responsibilities. When we slow down, we create time and space for reflection and evaluation of experiences, thoughts, and emotions, which is essential for personal growth (Kim, 2024). In her article, *Why "doing nothing, intentionally" is good for us: The rise of the slow living movement* (2024), author Holly Williams shares that #SlowLiving is on the rise with millennials. This could be because "millennials have been called a 'burnout generation' – and the combination of being raised to work hard in order to succeed, and then graduating with a mountain of debt into an unstable post-financial crash world has, as is well-documented, been a serious challenge for many" (n.p.). The realization that burnout in the millennial generation could potentially be a signal of hope that millennial educators and school leaders are ready to make necessary shifts in school demands.

Proactively working against speeding through our work, and instead replacing it with intentional slowness could be a changemaker in supporting our well-being. Strategically slowing down our pace can give us the chance to act thoughtfully, make connections, consider things deeply, and be present in the moment. It could give us the space to build relationships, uncover our authentic selves, and engage in the most meaningful work. Exploring the pace at which we are working could just be the secret key to unlocking all other aspects of our well-being.

Extending Compassion to Ourselves

Effective school leaders are generally empathetic and compassionate people. They will explore the reasoning behind a behavior or comment from a student, parent, or staff member. They will consider context and external factors, withholding judgment and listening to understand. They will extend trust and acknowledge the strengths and hard work of others. They understand mistakes are part of the process and will encourage others to keep trying. They value diversity and individuality, encouraging personal growth in a way that meets specific needs.

But it is a fair guess to say that this compassion may not always be extended to ourselves. We may be much more critical of ourselves, our actions, and our mistakes than we would ever dream of towards others. We potentially take failures and errors personally, resist self-forgiveness, and drive ourselves hard. It is in our human nature to be far harsher critics of ourselves than we ever would be of others, and so here may lie another key factor in the protection of our own well-being. Why do we do this to ourselves?

What could it look like, or feel like, if we could extend the same understanding and compassion to ourselves as we do for others? What if we could acknowledge that to be human is to be imperfect, and courageously move forward anyway? We know that others are more engaged and motivated when they are being treated with kindness and encouragement. Can we imagine speaking to ourselves in the same manner? How could that impact the effectiveness of our own work? If we could give ourselves the same grace that we do for others, we may well be in a better position to learn, grow, collaborate, and take care of ourselves.

This is not selfish behavior. This is not about relinquishing responsibility or indulging in self-pity. We recognize that for those who are habituated to self-criticism, it may in fact feel that way. It may be a habit that needs to be built from the ground up. Turning that critical inner voice to a more gentle, encouraging one may not be an easy path.

Self-compassion is courageous (Brierton, 3) and it is a powerful practice! Being kind to ourselves triggers oxytocin production, reduces anxiety, and counteracts cortisol levels from stress (Ketay et al, 2022). Self-compassion has the potential to make you a better leader as well (Fernandez & Stern, 2020). Rather than giving in to instinct by freezing or quitting when you make a mistake, being more empathetic with yourself means you are more likely to learn from your mistakes and move forward with your growth and development. It also means you are more likely to increase your compassion for others.

THE 5R's: REMEDYING STRATEGIES FOR YOUR WELL-BEING

▶ REIMAGINE

Power of Positive Emotions

It is time for us to reimagine the power of positive emotions. Positive emotions can reduce stress and burnout. But beyond just this, people with positive emotions are open to more possible actions, better planners, creative thinkers, and go-getters (Abdaal, 2023). Harnessing positive emotions goes far beyond just enjoying your day a little more. Feeling good can literally lead you to being more successful in your work.

We do not need to accept that work is tedious and unpleasant by design. We can build up these positive emotions and leverage them to feel good and improve our work performance. Consider what it is about your work that gives you these positive emotions. It might be from your interactions with others, in completing a task, tackling a new initiative, tracking growth, or creating a beautiful display. Recognize what it is for you that brings you positive emotions such as amusement, pride, hope, or interest. And then deliberately plan to bring as much of it as you can into your work. Leverage what feels good to support your well-being.

Boardman (2021) goes even further and describes engaging with positive feelings and activities as "emotional armor" (p. 65). Not only can these positive emotions enable you to work better, but they can actually serve as protection from future stressors, challenges, and inconveniences. Paying attention to and deliberately planning "uplifts," as Boardman describes them, can help you retrain negative thinking, being overly focused on deficits, and seeing threats all around us.

While it might seem a bit uncomfortable at first if you are not used to it, focusing on positive emotions can be a powerful factor in your well-being. Noticing positives, finding what feels good, appreciating what we have, and sharing this widely will be a superpower in your back pocket.

▶ REMOVE

The Concept of Well-Being as an Individual Responsibility

Burnout and stress are frequently viewed as an issue of the individual. It is time to remove this narrative. Burnout and stress are not the problem of the individual alone. More often than not it is due to systemic issues and structures. Dealing appropriately with burnout requires attending to workplace planning and problems. The top five causes of burnout are: unfair treatment at work, unmanageable workload, lack of role clarity, lack of communication/support from managers, and unreasonable time pressure (Moss, 2019). None of these are directly caused by the individual themselves. They also will not be solved overnight, as these issues take significant change to reverse the impact. It is unlikely that breathing practices, yoga, or a face mask will resolve issues when these root causes of burnout remain in place.

By removing the idea that it is the fault of the individual alone, we will also remove the added worry, guilt, or anxiety that you are the cause of the problem. Individuals that feel that they are somehow in deficit or at fault when they experience these issues will carry an extra burden. Remove this thinking, and take away that added extra unpleasant feeling standing in the way of healing and shifting to a healthier place.

The Stigma

As we highlight how the effects of stress and burnout are far beyond the fault of an individual, we also need to recognize the stigma that comes along with it. Unfortunately, even now, mental health challenges are often stigmatized. Those suffering from work-related stress may be seen to have characteristics that are inferior to others; their efforts and strengths discredited in the face of the issues they experience.

As we mention above, this stigma can add additional burdens to those who are already struggling to deal with their circumstances. But this is not where the problem with stigmas such as this ceases. When stigmas around stress and burnout continue, sufferers may not seek help or look for solutions as they would with other health concerns. Their symptoms may worsen as they continue working, or attempt to work harder to out-run the issues (Seppälä & King, 2017). The behavior and attention effects can spread outwards and impact the larger community.

The far-reaching effects of such stigmas can be overlooked. Building trusting relationships where we can broach the topic and model letting go of the stigma is important in removing this barrier. Recognizing that stigmas are still present and working to remove them is critical in effectively building well-being.

If you find yourselves stuck in negative thoughts to do with self-blame around stress and burnout, or the stigma associated with it, mindfulness practices may be helpful. Mindfulness practices that guide us to "let go" of uncomfortable thoughts have been found to be helpful in reducing rumination and in finding negative thoughts less intrusive (Hartnett & Carr, 2013). One such example of a "letting-go" practice is one known as "leaves on a stream."

To undertake this practice, find a comfortable position to sit or lie in. Imagine yourself sitting in a beautiful spot in nature alongside a stream. You watch as the water flows past you. It is a calm stream, with fresh, clear water gently bubbling along as it moves over river stones. Floating on the water are leaves that pass along and out of sight as the stream carries them down-river. As each troubling thought you have pops into your mind, attach it to a leaf, and watch as your thoughts are calmly carried away.

Engaging in mindfulness practices such as this may aid you in removing the added burden of negative rumination when you are struggling. Try it, or ones like it, regularly and see if it is a practice that works for you!

▶ REPURPOSE

Tired Notions of Self-Care

Tackling self-care for leaders can be a tempestuous topic. Some consider it a selfish thing to spend time on, when we have so many tasks to do and so many people to take care of. Others may consider it an unfair practice, handing over responsibility to an individual for something that should be embedded in system-wide practices. Perhaps it is something valuable for us to engage in, in order to be resilient in the face of the challenges we encounter in our work.

A simple search on the internet will give you endless lists of activities to pursue to engage in self-care. But the truth of the matter is that what works for one person will not necessarily work for everyone. What leaves one school leader feeling refreshed and ready to tackle another day may not even break the surface tension for another.

It is important that we all take note of what feels effective for ourselves in breaking that circuit of stress, and leaves us feeling recharged and reinvigorated. Self-care is not a one-size-fits-all situation and requires as much of a differentiated approach as our classrooms do. Being mindfully aware of what activities inside and outside the workplace lift us up and leave us feeling ready to keep going will help us to make a clear self-care plan for ourselves. And we need to make it a priority in order to keep bringing our best selves to our schools.

▶ REINVEST

Social Interactions

While school leaders may feel that they do not have the time or energy to invest in developing personal relationships, it is important to reinvest in cultivating these. We can see the research that shows that loneliness leads to depression, anxiety, as well as low life satisfaction. Mitigating the impact of the loneliness of leadership positions is vital to ensure maintenance of positive well-being (Kelly, 2019).

The relationships may be within school, within a PLC or network, or perhaps they need to be outside of work and the profession altogether. Perhaps it would be most helpful to develop relationships in conjunction with an outside hobby, or perhaps just with family members. A positive path forward may also be in team building with other members of the leadership team to build trust and understanding with those in a similar role. Wherever the source of relationships for you, resist the temptation to say you are too tired to socialize, and instead put the effort into these energizing interpersonal moments for a different type of well-being building.

▶ REFINE

Your Movement

Always moving at break-neck speed? Perhaps it is time to try principles of the slow movement and slow living. Do a reflection on your movements during your workweek. How do you feel when you are moving so quickly through your days? How about the days that feel slower and calmer? This is an area of your life that you can extend some compassion to yourself. Do you tell your friends or colleagues to slow down even when you are running at full speed?

Just as discussed in Chapter 5, moving constantly at such a high speed can have harmful effects on our physical and mental health, embracing an attitude of slowing down could be helpful in re-balancing your life. While the first step is recognizing that you are rushing endlessly, our work to mitigate this does not end there. Enlisting other strategies to slow down will be beneficial (Wellness Corner, 2023), including:

- Setting realistic goals.
- Practicing mindfulness.
- Establishing boundaries.
- Avoiding multitasking.
- Challenging perfectionism.
- Rereading Chapter 5 and the tips about editing your time!

Your Relationship with Sleep

Evaluating your sleep habits and giving sleep the credit it deserves will change your life. Just as we did in the above section, think about how you feel when you are rested versus when you are not. When you are rested, do you simply have the energy to engage with others in a more positive way than when you have had a night of fitful sleep? When Tammy does not sleep well, the first thing that pops in her mind in the morning is – "why do I have to people today?" This immediately illustrates the impact that sleep deprivation can have on our approach to our work. So let us examine some techniques that will help you get some more of that powerful, potent sleep energy back into your life.

Huffington's (2016) book has many tidbits and research-backed strategies to assist us with our sleep. While our schools might be a long way from having rooms dedicated to taking naps as she suggests (can you imagine!), there are still many achievable strategies that we can make use of in our lives. Her foundational tips include:

- Minimizing light (especially blue light) before bed.
- Keeping the temperature of your room cool overnight.
- Getting enough physical activity to embrace sleep.
- Remember that overindulging in caffeine and sugar throughout the day means being wired at night!

These ideas will be universally helpful to get the required sleep to be at our very best. Other avenues to explore depending on your personal preferences and experiences include ideas such as:

- Meditation.
- Breathing techniques.
- Mind dumping before bed.
- Gratitude practices.
- Drinking a sleepy tea before bed.
- Hot bath or shower before bed.
- Fitting in a nap or two when you can!

We really cannot overestimate the impact that sleep can have on our well-being. Whatever way works for you, aim to refine your approach and make it a priority in your life. Every aspect of your well-being will thank you!

LINGERING QUESTIONS

- What are the activities that I engage in that help me feel recharged, and how can I fit more into my life?
- What routine or schedule can I set up that will keep me consistent with focusing on my well-being?
- Once I feel like I have a good set of routines and strategies to support my well-being, how can I ensure that I continue to sustain them over the long term?

In our final chapter, we move into our concluding thoughts. We review our key messages from the book and leave you with our parting thoughts and wishes for moving forward.

References

Abdaal, A. (2023). *Feel good productivity: How to do more of what matters to you*. Penguin Life.

Beausaert, S., Froehlich, D. E., Riley, P., & Gallant, A. (2021). What about school principals' well-being? The role of social capital. *Journal of Educational Administration*. https://www.researchgate.net/publication/349281816_What_about_school_principals'_well-being_The_role_of_social_capital

Blankson, A. (2022, October 24). The rise of the slow productivity movement. *Forbes*. https://www.forbes.com/sites/amyblankson/2022/10/24/the-rise-of-the-slow-productivity-movement/

Boardman, J. (2021, April). Chronic stress: The health impact of persistent frustrations. *The Psychologist, 34*. https://thepsychologist.bps.org.uk/volume-34/april-2021/chronic-stress-health-impact-persistent-frustrations

Brierton, K. (2023). *Healthy School: The key role of compassionate leadership*. Global Compassion Coalition. https://www.globalcompassioncoalition.org/healthy-schools-the-key-role-of-compassionate-leadership/

Fernandez, R., & Stern, S. (2020, November 9). Self-compassion will make you a better leader. *Harvard Business Review*. https://hbr.org/2020/11/self-compassion-will-make-you-a-better-leader

Gacherieu, D. R. (2024, May/June). Why principals stay. *Leadership, The Association of California School Administrators*. https://leadership.acsa.org/why-principals-stay

Geraghty, T. (n.d.). Edgar Schein's three layers of organizational culture. *Psychological Safety*. https://psychsafety.co.uk/psychological-safety-edgar-scheins-three-layers-of-organisational-culture/

Hartnett, D., & Carr, A. (2013). Letting go and mindfulness: A review and a call for research. *Clinical Child Psychology and Psychiatry, 18*(3), 424–439. https://doi.org/10.1177/1359104512455814

Harvard School of Public Health, Robert Wood Johnson Foundation, & NPR. (2014). *The burden of stress in America*. https://media.npr.org/documents/2014/july/npr_rwjf_harvard_stress_poll.pdf

Huffington, A. (2016). *The sleep revolution: Transforming your life, one night at a time*. Harmony Books.

Kelly, H. (2019, March 17). The loneliness of the international school leader. *The International Educator*. https://www.tieonline.com/article/2500/the-loneliness-of-the-international-school-leader

Kelly, H. (2023). *School leaders matter: Preventing burnout, managing stress, and improving wellbeing*. Routledge.

Ketay, S., Beck, L. A., & Dejci, J. (2022). Self-compassion and social stress: Links with subjective stress and cortisol responses. *Self and Identity, 22*(3), 486–505. https://www.tandfonline.com/doi/full/10.1080/15298868.2022.2117733

Kim, A. (2024). *The slow life: Embracing stillness in a fast-paced world*. Mindful Living Press.

McKeown, G. (2014). *Essentialism: The disciplined pursuit of less*. Crown Business.

Moss, J. (2019, December). Burnout is about your workplace, not your people. *Harvard Business Review*. https://hbr.org/2019/12/burnout-is-about-your-workplace-not-your-people

Musiowsky-Borneman, T., & Arnold, C. (2024, February 21). *Episode 053: The slow schools movement with Tammy and Christine* [Audio podcast episode]. In *The Minimalist Educator Podcast* (No. 053). Apple Podcasts. https://podcasts.apple.com/dz/podcast/episode-053-the-slow-schools-movement-with/id1705945605?i=1000679070749

National Association of Secondary School Principals. (2022). *[NASSP's Survey of America's School Leaders and High School Students]*. https://survey.nassp.org/2022/

Perry, B. D., & Hambrick, E. P. (2008). The neurosequential model of therapeutics. *Reclaiming Children and Youth, 17*(3), 38–43.

Seppälä, E., & King, M. (2017, June). Burnout at work isn't just about exhaustion. It's also about loneliness. *Harvard Business Review*. https://hbr.org/2017/06/burnout-at-work-isnt-just-about-exhaustion-its-also-about-loneliness

Sonnentag, S., Cheng, B. H., & Parker, S. L. (2022). Recovery from work: Advancing the field toward the future. *Annual Review of Organizational Psychology and Organizational Behavior, 9*(1), 33–60. https://www.annualreviews.org/docserver/fulltext/orgpsych/9/1/annurev-orgpsych-012420-091355.pdf

TES. (n.d.). *TES Wellbeing Report*. https://www.tes.com/for-schools/content/tes-wellbeing-report

Wellness Corner. (2023). *How to stop rushing and start living mindfully*. https://www.wellnesscorner.com/blog/how-to-stop-rushing

Williams, H. (2024, January 3). Why "doing nothing, intentionally" is good for us: The rise of the slow living movement. *BBC*. https://www.bbc.com/worklife/article/20240102-why-doing-nothing-intentionally-is-good-for-us-the-rise-of-the-slow-living-movement

Chapter 8
Concluding Thought for Moving into Action

Throughout this book we have been walking through and discussing ideas, principles, mindsets, and behaviors that can make or break a culture of less in a school. As we wrap up our discussions, strategy suggestions, and ideas for support in editing your leadership role, we want to return to our earlier thoughts from previous chapters.

We borrowed ideas from our focus on purpose, priorities, and paring down from *The Minimalist Teacher* (2021) and have shared discussions about the realities of large scale school systems. We took those discussions and further worked through strategies for how we can reimagine, remove, repurpose, reinvest, and refine what we do in our schools to support a strategic declutter and edit of the high-level systems that drive a school.

We challenge you to rethink the perceptions you have about your role and your place in it. We challenge you to reimagine the expectations that you set upon yourself and that others may have of you. And we challenge you to be kind to yourself in light of all the responsibilities you have chosen to take on.

In the first chapter, "Creating a Mindset and Culture for a Leadership Edit," we were examining how to prepare and build a mindset and culture for living in an ecosystem where minimalism, clarity, and focus are valued. The intent is that all staff and school community members understand the importance of making school a place in which all structures and systems are intentionally planned and reviewed not only by school leaders, but collectively. School leadership is a tough place to be and developing the capacity in the entire school community supports the work that leaders do. Doing strategically less benefits all staff. When we are prioritized and focused, we can maintain a level of mental clarity that elevates the level of work we can do in our roles. This elevated level of work keeps our focus on student learning and supporting teacher development. This is why we do what we do. We are in the industry of developing people and we can do this when we all understand that what we do has meaning.

In "Editing Communication," we discussed cultural aspects of communication, directionality, and purpose by identifying ways to clarify messaging for intended audiences. We discussed the frustrations and mistrust that stem from unclear communication and introduced how to refocus on relationships as a foundation for building strong communication. The 5R's strategies were shared as a support for you to edit and enrich your communication plans and processes to ensure that you and your team are effectively communicating with your community members.

In "Editing Expectations," we focused our discussion on the complex expectation systems that form the structure of a school. We focused on decluttering and editing the development and implementation of schoolwide expectation structures such as strategic plans, accreditation, and goal setting. The 5R's strategies were provided to support the reflection of these structures and to rethink schoolwide expectations and plans effectively. This creates a clear purpose and vision for supporting a strong school ecosystem.

In "Editing Educator Support," we discussed the processes such as mentoring, coaching, observation cycles, and evaluations that are meant to support teachers in improving practice and the clutter that can create complications and lack of trust in the process. We provided some structures in the 5R's to ensure that trust is developed and relationships are supported in this context. This is to create a system of a continuous cycle of growth and improvement, keeping engagement and motivation high, and can evolve into a more effective teacher support structure.

In "Editing Your Time Structures," we provided discussion about our understanding of time, strategies we have tried over time that may have been a relatable point for you, and the reality of actual time expenditure on tasks, responsibilities, and minutia in a leadership role. We dove into the real and overwhelming concern that many educators feel the burden of "not enough time" and provided some respite for that worry. Strategies within the 5R's were intended to support you in your leadership role by reconceptualizing how you can sort out your time spend, remove distractions, and think about how to more effectively use time to meet (or not meet) with staff.

In "Editing Family Participation," we considered how family participation supports student success. Research points to involvement and engagement within the school community as a vital element for a student's success and developing a strong school community. Yet attempts to develop a good relationship with families can fail. Here we considered the 5R's to look at involvement and engagement by placing value on diversity, understanding perspectives and parent strengths, and evaluating ways for removing barriers to authentic engagement.

In "Remedy Your Well-Being," we discussed the trap of the martyrdom-adjacent experience that many school leaders live every day. We focused discussion on the inconsequential amount of attention that is given to the well-being of our school leaders. By focusing discussion on how school leaders can do well in the roles AND preserve their mental and physical health, we can shift some of the unhealthy ideas that school leaders do not need the support and well-being development because of the roles they hold, because "you can handle it." Strategies shared in the 5R's section provide some more reconceptualization of what school leader well-being is and means.

This short review might remind you of how much your role entails, that you are capable, and that it is okay that you may not always have the capacity. Relying on your staff and leadership team to support the process of leading a school and strengthening your ability to care for yourself will benefit your community in the long term.

▶ ACCOUNTABILITY AND ADVOCACY MEASURES

You will only see the change you want to experience if you take action starting on a small scale and advocate for it on a broader scale. It will always be advantageous to you to have an advocacy plan and an accountability partner or group to work on strategically creating space in your role.

Find your people if you do not yet have a professional learning network. You may have a leadership team at your school and you may be supported by a team in your district you connect with. We strongly suggest finding an additional network outside of your building or district to gain a broader perspective on the work of a school leader. Regardless of who is in your network, everyone in the group needs to understand the parameters of each other's roles and think through how to offer the best support possible to each other. Determine who in your network will be your accountability folks. Who will check in with you when you have that report to write and send to the superintendent? Who will you check in with when you are feeling overwhelmed? Who will be the one who can accept your early morning texts when there is an emergency?

Here we invite you to think about the connection between taking action, advocacy, and accountability. Each of these components is necessary in bringing your editing process to life for a more sustainable leadership experience (Figure 8.1–8.3).

Just as you have planned this for yourself, you will encourage your accountability partners or team to do the same so you can fill in your name for reciprocal check-ins. Be kind and firm with each other as this accountability process is critical to the maintenance of your newly edited systems and structures.

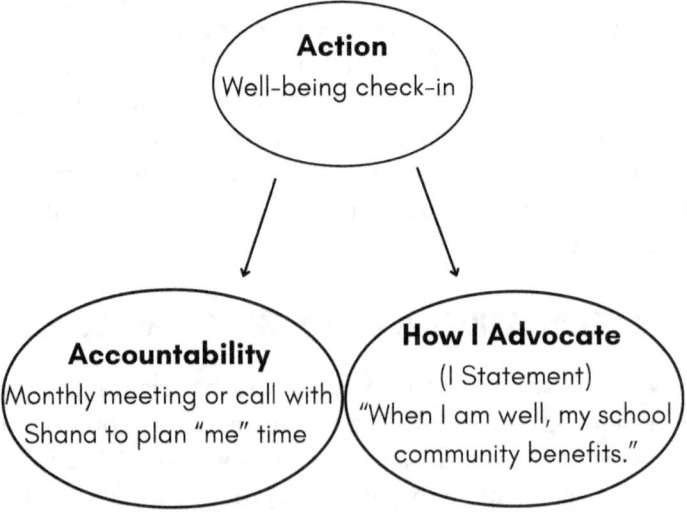

Figure 8.1 Accountability Web for Well-Being

Concluding Thought for Moving into Action

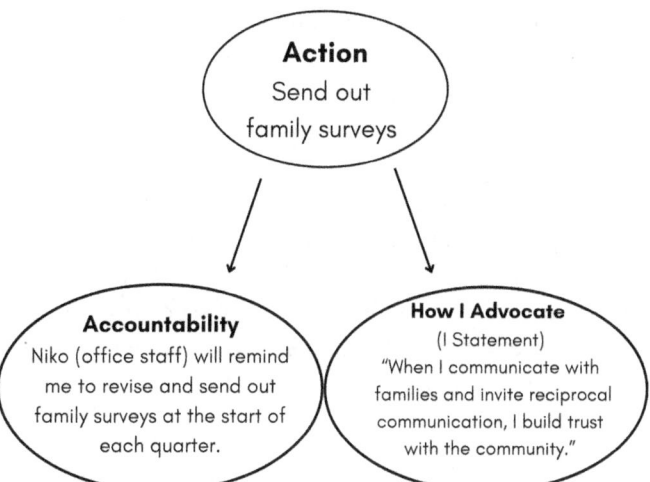

Figure 8.2 Accountability Web for Family Communication

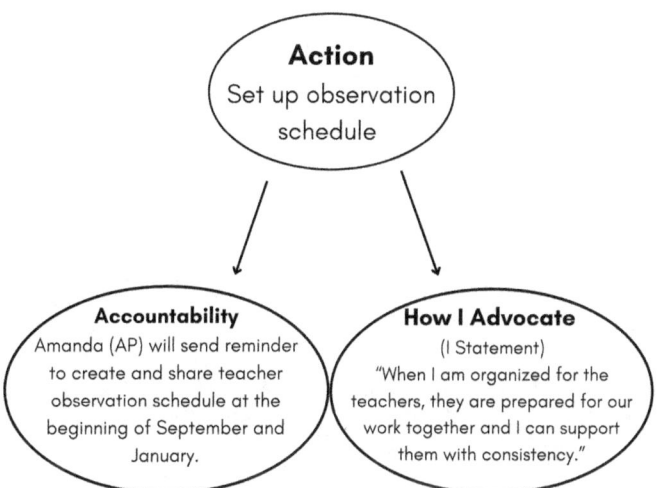

Figure 8.3 Accountability Web for Teacher Support

▶ MOVING FORWARD USING THE 5R's

As we wrap up this book, we wish for you to move forward with intentionality and focus. You are the model for effectiveness and efficiency, and you can always:

- rethink what and how you lead processes and systems,
- remove the friction,

- repurpose the old systems and artifacts to make them new,
- reinvest in your people and resources, and
- refine your existing systems and actions to make them more efficient and purposeful.

Remember your influence. You have the capability to shift mindsets, systems, actions, and words to be more strategic and sustainable. We wish you prosperity and calm while you work through your processes of decluttering and editing your school's systems in the efforts to create an ecosystem in which all of your community members can thrive, including you.

For Product Safety Concerns and Information please contact our EU representative GPSR@taylorandfrancis.com
Taylor & Francis Verlag GmbH, Kaufingerstraße 24, 80331 München, Germany

www.ingramcontent.com/pod-product-compliance
Lightning Source LLC
Chambersburg PA
CBHW070258230426
43664CB00014B/2568